DEDICATION

This book is lovingly dedicated to all those who are seeking a deeper, more intimate relationship with God. To those who truly want an encounter with Him that will take them past head knowledge into an experience of intimacy, power, and transformation.

Ancient Secrets
of the
Tabernacle Revealed

Your Pathway to God's Presence

—— ∞ ——

BY DAVID CERULLO

TABLE OF CONTENTS

AN INVITATION TO INTIMACY

The Journey

*W*E'RE ABOUT TO EMBARK together on an incredible journey—one I'm convinced will transform your life and bring you into a new level of relationship, intimacy, and power with God as you've never experienced before. Something very special, very unique, awaits you as you journey through the pages of this book with me.

The very fact that you have picked up this book and begun to read it is evidence God has something special on His mind for you. Your heavenly Father has scheduled this time—made this appointment with you—to reveal hidden mysteries in the pictures and patterns of His Word that will bring you to a special place where He's been waiting for you.

As we walk this path together, please consider me both a student of the Word and a guide for this journey. I'm not the teacher. I certainly don't have all the answers and don't understand all the hidden mysteries of Scripture, but I've uncovered some amazing things I'm going to share with you.

In my personal journey with God, I've learned there are mysteries and revelations hidden in His Word—mysteries He's placed there for you and me to search out. There are patterns of God and pictures within His Word—not just words on paper but pictures He wants us to see.

As Proverbs 25:2 says, *"It is the glory of God to conceal a thing: But the honor of kings is to search out a matter"*(KJV). So we're about to embark on a treasure hunt together. True riches and treasures aren't found lying around on the ground in plain sight. Whether you're searching for silver, gold, or precious stones, you have to dig for them, mine for them, and search for them. As a side note, when you read the Bible, look for pictures, follow the patterns, and they will reveal mysteries God has hidden in His Word.

One thing is certain: Understanding God and all the mysteries and revelations of His word are inexhaustible. The more I learn or the more I think I know, the more I discover I don't know. There's always more. I'm reminded of John 21:25 where the Bible says of the things Jesus did, *"I suppose that even the world itself would not contain the books that would be written."* The journey we're about to take is like that...inexhaustible.

THE POWER IN FIVE WORDS

Many years ago, I was reading in Philippians 3 where the apostle Paul expressed his passionate desire to know God more. I'll share more of my story about this in the pages to come, but I want you to know that this Scripture passage set me on a journey that continues to change my life.

God dropped five words into my spirit that day. As I began to "search out the matter," the Holy Spirit led me to an unusual Scripture in Ezekiel that seemed to just jump off the page at me. You know what I'm talking about; I'm sure it's happened to you. You're reading the Word when all of a sudden, a particular Scripture passage or verse grabs your attention in a way it never did before.

For me, that scripture was Ezekiel 43:10 and 11 (KJV), *"Thou son of man, show the house to the house of Israel, that they may be ashamed of their iniquities: and let them measure the pattern. And if they be ashamed of all that they have done, show them the form of the house...and write it in their sight, that they may keep the whole form thereof, and all the ordinances thereof, and do them."*

God was saying to Ezekiel, *"Show My house (the Temple) to the house of Israel (my people), describe it to them, help them to understand everything about it and its meaning and help them to see how far away from My pattern they've wandered."*

This is like a person trying to make a garment from a pattern and a piece of cloth. Unless you have a pattern to place on top of the cloth, chances are you won't make the garment to the right dimensions and it will be unwearable.

With those five words I felt God drop into my spirit–and with this passage from Ezekiel–I started a journey that has taken me to places with the Lord I never thought imaginable. I began studying the Tabernacle before diving into a study of the Temple.

I'm still learning and uncovering hidden mysteries along the way, and I won't try to share with you everything I've learned so far in this one book, but I will tell you this: Every part of the Tabernacle had purpose, meaning, stories to tell, and mysteries to reveal. There are historical, prophetical, and practical applications for us today.

(For example, hidden in the pattern, pictures, and mysteries of the Tabernacle and the Temple are prophetic revelations of how long the "age of the law" would be. That's the period of time from when God gave Moses the Ten Commandments on the top of Mount Sinai until the Messiah would come. Both the Tabernacle and the Temple patterns describe how long the "age of grace", would last, which is the time period between the end of the Law, the beginning of grace, and the time frame when the Father sends His Son back to rapture the Church. There's even a picture of the millennial reign of Christ on this earth in the patterns of the Tabernacle and Temple!)

For right now, we're going to take a journey together on a pathway to discover practical and experiential truths and mysteries hidden in the pictures and patterns of the Tabernacle, the priestly duties, and the furniture itself.

I believe the revelations of the mysteries of the Tabernacle are some of the greatest revelations in the entire Bible of God, of His Son, of the pathway to His very presence and the life-changing, transforming relationship we can enjoy with Him.

Let's get started!

AN INVITATION TO INTIMACY

"The heavens are telling of the glory of God; and their expanse is declaring the work of His hands."

I'm sure you've looked up into the night sky more than once and wondered about the incredible universe God has created. I do often. Whenever I gaze into the stars, the verse from Psalm 144:3 comes to mind, *"O LORD, what is man, that You take knowledge of him? Or the son of man, that You think of him?"*

I love astronomy. I find it fascinating. With all of our science and technology, man hasn't been able to measure the extent of the cosmos. Astronomers speculate that there are literally billions of galaxies. David wrote in Psalm 19:1, *"The heavens are telling of the glory of God; And their expanse is declaring the work of His hands."* That's one thing most scientists and astronomers agree on...the universe is expanding just as God's Word says it is.

I don't know if you've ever taken a look at the size of our planet Earth in comparison to some of the other planets in our solar system. While the earth is larger than Venus, Mars, Mercury, or Pluto, we dwarf in comparison to Neptune, Uranus, Saturn, or Jupiter.

Just take a look on the following pages:

If it looks like Jupiter, the largest planet in our solar system is big, compare that to our sun.

If you think our sun looks big, compare that to Arcturus.

Or compare Arcturus to Betelgeuse or Antares.

My point simply is that in all of God's magnificent creation...in the entire expanse of the universe...here is planet Earth where God made man, and in the midst of all that, the God of the universe wants to have a personal, intimate relationship with you and me. Incredible. Amazing. Unbelievable.

What is man that God is mindful of us?

God created you and me for fellowship and relationship. The Garden of Eden was a place where God Himself would come down to walk and talk with Adam and Eve. God gave them dominion over the earth and told them to be fruitful and multiply (Genesis 9:7). Earth was created to be their dwelling place, and the Garden of Eden was a place God came and "dwelt" with man.

Years later God would speak to Moses and say in Exodus 25:8 *"Let them construct a sanctuary for Me, that I may dwell among them."* The purpose of the Tabernacle was to be a dwelling place for God on the earth.

And this incredible, amazing, indescribable God wants to dwell—to tabernacle—with *you.* That's why understanding the Tabernacle is so important to us. Hidden within are pictures, patterns, and mysteries—revelations of how to approach His presence.

THE TABERNACLE

When King David was just a shepherd boy tending his father's sheep, no doubt he looked up into these same night skies that hold Jupiter, Arcturus, and Antares, and in awe, wonderment, and amazement communed and fellowshipped with God. God referred to him as *"a man after His own heart"* (1 Samuel 13:14). During those isolated months and years spent in the fields, young David developed a relationship with the Lord characterized by worship and intimacy.

Years later, after he had been made king over Israel, David brought the Ark of the Covenant to Jerusalem and established the city as the center of worship for the Most High God. Because the Temple had

Mercury

Venus

Mars

Earth

Sizes in relation to Earth's surrounding planets

Jupiter

Mercury

Earth

Venus

Mars

Sun

Saturn

Pluto

Uranus

Neptune

Planet sizes in relation to the Sun

Star sizes in relation to the Sun

Pollux

Sirius

Sun

Arcturus

Stars in relation to Antares

Arcturus

Sirius

Pollux

Arcturus

Antares

Aldebaran

Rigel

yet been built, David set up a temporary tabernacle to house the
rk and ordained priests to minister there before the Lord.

Imagine how overcome with emotion David must have been
when the prophet Nathan declared that God was going to establish
His Kingdom through David's lineage *forever.* After he heard this
prophecy, Scripture says that David immediately *"went in and sat
before the Lord"* and poured out his heart to God (1 Chronicles 17).

Where did David go to sit before the Lord? The TABERNACLE.
Overcome by a sense of worship, humility, and awe over God's goodness
and mercy, David wanted to draw as near to Him as possible.

As the sunlight shone through the walls of the tent, it would
have cast a shadow over the Ark of the Covenant, and I can just see
David crawling into the shadow of the cherubims' wings, desperately
trying to draw as close as he could to the presence of the Lord without
touching the Ark. The cry of His heart was, *"Hide me in the shadow of
Your wings"* (Psalm 17:8).

Like King David, you and I were created to live in intimacy with
God, Who desires to have an intensely personal relationship with each

of us. But exactly what does it *mean* to have an intimate relationship with Him?

We can say that we *truly* know someone and they *truly* know us only when we know the other person's deepest thoughts, emotions, and responses. Feelings of closeness, calm, and comfort characterize the relationship. In the same way, this is what it's like to have an intimate relationship with the Lord.

The word "intimate" comes from the Latin word *intimus* meaning "close friend." The verb is *intimare*, which means "to make known." To be intimate with someone means to be a close friend, one who is willing to risk making himself or herself known by being open and vulnerable.

God wants us to love and trust Him so much that we invite Him to see into the deepest parts of our lives and hearts, even those parts we tend to hide from Him in fear and shame. He wants us to share ourselves fully with Him and receive His love, just as He desires to share Himself fully with us and receive our love.

I love the picture of intimacy painted for us in the old hymn, "In the Garden":

> *I come to the garden alone, while the dew is still on the roses,*
> *And the voice I hear falling on my ear,*
> *the Son of God discloses.*
> *And He walks with me,*
> *and He talks with me,*
> *And He tells me I am His own;*
> *And the joy we share as we tarry there,*
> *none other has ever known.*

AUSTIN MILES, 191

In recent years, God has shown me how an intimate rel
with Him enables us to live powerful, peace-filled, overc
while having a greater impact in the world for Jesus C
Kingdom. Our hunger for Him will take us into the ri
where *"deep calls to deep"* (Psalm 42:7).

Wh' the day finally comes that I meet Jes'

want to just hear Him say, *"Well done, good and faithful servant."* I want to be able to run into His outstretched arms and hear Him whisper, *"I love you, and I know you love Me. Welcome home."* This is the kind of intimate relationship the Lord desires to have with *you.*

My prayer is that this book will serve as a treasure map to help you discover the pathway leading to an ever-deepening intimacy with God. I invite you now to journey with me on this pathway leading to His heart.

> *"I will open my mouth with a parable; I will utter*
>
> *hidden things, things from of old."*
>
> PSALM 78:2 (NIV)

David

PART 1

The Pathway to His Presence

CHAPTER 1

Missing the Mark

"You are in Christ Jesus,

who became to us wisdom from God,

and righteousness and sanctification, and redemption."

1 CORINTHIANS 1:30

*W*HETHER WE REALIZE IT or not, every one of us is crying out for more of God's presence. Something inside us yearns to know Him, to experience intimacy with Him, and to offer the only thing we truly have to give Him...our worship.

My own journey into intimacy with the Lord began many years ago with a growing cry in my heart for a deeper, more intimate relationship with Him.

I was sitting in a hotel room, preparing a message I was to deliver that evening at a conference. I was reading Philippians 3 when I came across this verse written by the apostle Paul: *"...that I may know Him and the power of His resurrection"* (v. 10).

I was blown away when I read those words. I thought, "Paul how could *you* possibly say this? You wrote two-thirds of the N Testament, and *you're* talking about wanting to know God? If *you* like *you* didn't know God, who else could possibly know Him?"

Then the realization dawned that all of us are on a journey heart of God, and none of us will arrive at the end of this until we're in Heaven. None of us is at the place of intima where He desires us to be. Paul was simply saying that he wasn't yet where God was calling him to be in his relationship with Him, but he was pressing upward toward the call of God in Christ Jesus.

I was desperately hungry to know God like this, and so I prayed, "Lord, I want to know You. I don't want just to know *about* You…I want to *know* You."

I then heard the Lord speak to my spirit: *"David, do you want to go to that next level with Me…beyond acquaintance, beyond friendship, beyond knowing about Me? Are you truly longing for a deeper level of relationship?"*

I responded, "Yes, Lord, I truly want an intimate relationship with You."

He replied, *"David, if you really want to get to know Me, why aren't you spending more time with Me?"* Now, let me be honest with you. When God asked me this, it hurt. Actually, it hurt a lot. I did spend time with the Lord, but He was gently and firmly convicting me that I usually limited my time with Him because of my overcrowded schedule.

He continued, *"We don't talk very much. You don't spend much time in My presence. If you truly want to know Me, you're going to need to spend more time with Me."*

I thought about this for a while. There are a lot of ways we can get to know someone. Often when we meet someone for the first time, we've already heard *about* them, but we don't really *know* them. The only way we get to know someone is by spending TIME with them.

All of us have different kinds of relationships on different levels with different people…

- There are people we've only heard about but will never know.
  There are people we've met, but we don't invest any time with them, so we'll never *really* get to know them.
  There are people we spend more time with and get to know a little bit.

And then there are those with whom we spend a lot of time, those who eventually become our closest and most intimate friends.

The more time we invest in our relationship with someone, the more we know them and the closer we become. This is why the first thing the Lord said to me when I prayed for a more intimate relationship with Him was, *"If you want to truly know Me, spend time with Me."*

And so I did.

Later that morning, I went down to the hotel restaurant to get some breakfast. As I was sitting there drinking my coffee and considering what God had said about how I needed to spend more time with Him, I sensed He was about to speak to my spirit again. I fished an envelope and a pen out of my pocket to write down whatever He was about to tell me.

*"David, if you truly want to know Me, there are some **STEPS** you're going to need to take in order to move into a deeper level of relationship with Me."*

"Yes, Lord. I'll take these steps. Whatever they are, I'll take them." And I quickly scrawled on the envelope the five words the Lord spoke to me:

"REPENT. PRAISE. WORSHIP. OFFERING. SACRIFICE."

Little did I know the impact these words would have on my life over the next several years.

MISSING THE MARK

The first step God said I would need to take if I wanted to know Him more intimately was

"REPENT.

PRAISE.

WORSHIP.

OFFERING.

SACRIFICE."

"*Repent.*" Ouch! That was a tough word for me to hear.

But I understood why He was saying this to me. As Believers, so many times we knock on God's door, wanting to spend time with Him when we haven't prepared ourselves to enter into His Holy presence. The psalmist David wrote:

"*Who may ascend into the hill of the LORD? And who may stand in His holy place? He who has clean hands and a pure heart, who has not lifted up his soul to falsehood and has not sworn deceitfully. He shall receive a blessing from the LORD and righteousness from the God of his salvation*" (Psalm 24:3-5).

When we ask Jesus Christ to be our Lord and Savior, we are immediately washed clean by His blood. Our sins are forgiven, and His righteousness becomes our righteousness: "*...You are in Christ Jesus, who became to us wisdom from God, and righteousness and sanctification, and redemption*" (1 Corinthians 1:30).

However, when the disciples asked Jesus to teach them to pray, He told them to pray these words as part of their *daily* prayer: "*And forgive us our debts* [sins], *as we also have forgiven our debtors* [those who have sinned against us]" (Matthew 6:12). Although inviting Jesus to be the Lord of our life cleanses us from our sin nature, He taught that we must still repent for our sins on a daily basis.

But exactly what is sin? The Greek word for sin is *hamartia*, which means "to miss the mark." Sin is anything we do or fail to do where we "miss the mark" of God's standard of holiness. And most of us "miss the mark" repeatedly throughout the day!

This is why Jesus taught that we need to ask God's forgiveness for ʌr sins daily. Thoughts that shouldn't have been entertained, words ˙ shouldn't have been spoken, actions we shouldn't have done, or ˙s not taken that God wanted us to do...all these occur in our lives ˙y basis. Having "*clean hands and a pure heart*" in order to spend ˙me with the Lord requires us to repent for our daily sins.

ʌrd "repent" comes from the Greek word *metaneo*, and ʌs "to think differently." True repentance ʌequires

Having clean hands

and a pure heart

in order to spend intimate time

with the Lord requires us

to repent for our daily sins.

changing your mind about your sin, and then changing your thinking and your behavior. Refusing or avoiding repentance for our sin actually prevents us from having an intimate relationship with the Lord.

Psalms 66:18 reminds us, *"If I regard wickedness in my heart, the Lord will not hear me,"* and Isaiah 59:1-2 sobers us with this warning: *"But your iniquities have made a separation between you and your God, and your sins have hidden His face from you so that He does not hear."*

Now please understand, I'm not saying God requires us to be perfect. He doesn't. He knows we're weak and vulnerable to temptation. But what I *am* saying is that God has provided us with an escape from His judgment for our sin: repentance based on faith in Jesus Christ *alone*, both initially when we're forgiven once and for all for our sin nature, and then forgiveness for the sins we daily commit that will block us from knowing Him intimately.

Genuine repentance before God is a sign of our brokenness and our desperation for Him.

"Be gracious to me, O God, according to Your lovingkindness; According to the greatness of Your compassion blot out my transgressions. Wash me thoroughly from my iniquity and cleanse me from my sin...The sacrifices of God are a broken spirit; A broken and a contrite heart, O God, You will not despise" (Psalm 51:1-2, 17).

God is so glad when we humble ourselves before Him to repent for our sins. He lovingly forgives us and welcomes us into His presence as we ask for His power to strengthen and help us when we "miss the mark."

REJOICING ANGELS

want to pause here for a moment and speak directly to the person ading this book right now who has never repented before God for · sinful nature and invited Jesus Christ to be their Lord and Savior. you're reading this book, I'm assuming it's because you're for an intimate relationship with Him. However, until Jesus d of your life, you can *never* experience intimacy with God.

Because God is holy, and the *only* way to come into His presence is to be made holy once and for all by the Blood of the One who never sinned—Jesus Christ.

Only by accepting that His death on the Cross is the one true way leading to God do we, *"have confidence to enter the holy place by the blood of Jesus"* (Hebrews 10:19).

But the good news is that you don't have to wait any longer! You can repent for your sinful nature right now and *immediately* have the awesome right to an intimate relationship with God, Who loves you with an everlasting love that will never fail! All you have to do is...

1. **Acknowledge you're a sinner.** *"For all have sinned and fall short of the glory of God"* (Romans 3:23).

2. **Confess your sins.** *"If we confess our sins, He is faithful and righteous to forgive us our sins and to cleanse us from all unrighteousness"* (1 John 1:9).

3. **Repent ("change your mind") for your sins.** *"Let the wicked forsake his way, and the unrighteous man his thoughts: and let him return to the LORD, and He will have compassion on him; and to our God, for He will abundantly pardon"* (Isaiah 55:7).

4. **Believe that Jesus is God's Son and lived a sinless life, yet chose to die a sinner's death on the Cross to save you from your sins.** *"If you confess with your mouth Jesus as Lord, and believe in your heart that God raised Him from the dead, you will be saved; for with the heart a person believes, resulti_ in righteousness, and with the mouth he confe_ resulting in salvation"* (Romans 10:9-10).

5. Pray this simple prayer:

Heavenly Father, Thank You for Your great love for me. I confess that I am a sinner. I repent of my sins and ask You to please forgive me. I believe that Jesus Christ is Your Son, that He died on the Cross for me, and that You raised Him from the dead. Please wash me clean with His blood. Thank You for forgiving me and making me Your child.

Jesus, please come into my life right now, live in my heart, and fill me with Your Holy Spirit. Be my Savior and Lord. Set me free now from every bondage the devil has held in my life.

Jesus, I pray this prayer in Your powerful Name. *Amen.*

If you just prayed this prayer, then welcome to the family of God! Right now, the angels in Heaven are rejoicing over you (Luke 15:10), and I'm rejoicing over you too!

In the following days, weeks, and months, you will sense the Lord drawing you into an increasingly intimate relationship. Talk to Him. Read His Word. Fellowship with other Believers. Spend time every day with Him. He loves you so much and wants to be with you. And keep reading this book to discover powerful treasures that will help you draw closer and closer to Him.

Remember...the daily confession of our sins is a powerful step e can take in our journey toward intimacy with God. As we come re Him, washed and cleansed by Jesus' Blood and the mercy of forgiveness, we're ready to take the next step that will take us into His presence.

DIGGING DEEPER

1. Think about a person with whom you have had a close, loving, intimate relationship. What made this relationship special and different from other relationships in your life?

2. Compared to the relationship you just described in #1, how would you like your relationship with the Lord to be the same or different?

3. Consider when your relationship with the Lord first began. How has it changed, strengthened, or weakened since then?

4. Spend some time with the Lord and ask Him to reveal areas of your life where you are "missing the mark." When He reveals any sin, simply repent. Tell Him you have "changed your mind" and that with His courage, grace, and strength, you also will change your thinking and your behavior.

CHAPTER TWO

Stones Can't Praise Him

"Great is the Lord,

and highly to be praised."

PSALM 145:3

*T*HE NEXT STEP GOD ASKED me to take in my journey toward a more intimate relationship with Him was *"PRAISE."* Although praise had always been an important aspect of my relationship with the Lord, He was asking me to make this a priority in our time together. I nodded in agreement, realizing that after repentance, praise is the key to unlocking the gateway to God's presence.

Since praising God helps lead us to a place of intimacy, it's important we understand exactly what praise is.

Psalm 100:4 declares, *"Enter His gates with thanksgiving and His courts with **praise**. Give thanks to Him, bless His name."* The Hebrew word for "praise" used in this verse is *tehillah,* which means "celebration; lauding someone or something that is worthy." When we praise God, we're celebrating His goodness and declaring truths about His worthiness. We celebrate Him for what He has done, what He is doing, and what He will do. With our praise, we acknowledge His greatness:

"Every day I will bless You, and I will praise Your name forever and ever. Great is the LORD, and highly to be praised, and His greatness is unsearchable. One generation shall praise Your works to another, and shall declare Your mighty acts.

"On the glorious splendor of Your majesty and on Your wonderful works, I will meditate. Men shall speak of the power of Your awesome acts, and I will tell of Your greatness" (Psalm 145:2-6).

Praising God also inevitably includes thanksgiving:

"Give thanks to the LORD, for He is good, for His lovingkindness is everlasting. Give thanks to the God of gods, for His lovingkindness is everlasting. Give thanks to the Lord of lords, for His lovingkindness is everlasting. To Him who alone does great wonders, for His lovingkindness is everlasting" (Psalm 136:1-4).

Our praise for God is based on His greatness and not on our emotions. We can *choose* to praise Him, regardless of how we're feeling. When the psalmist was overwhelmed with despair, he COMMANDED his soul to praise God and put hope in Him: *"Why are you in despair, O my soul? And why are you disturbed within me? Hope in God, for I shall again praise Him, the help of my countenance and my God"* (Psalm 43:5).

WHY DO WE PRAISE GOD?

Some might ask, "Well, *why* should I praise God?" That's a great question, and it's one clearly answered in Scripture. Our praise for God...

- **Declares** His worthiness! (Psalm 48:1; 145:3; Revelation 4:11; 5:12)
- **Demonstrates** our obedience! (Psalm 150:1; 81:1-4)
- **Defeats** our enemies! (Psalm 8:1-2; 18:1-3; 46-49)
- **Delivers** us from afflictions! (Psalm 34:4-8; 108:5-6)
- **Defies** our circumstances! (Psalm 116)

We don't praise God because of *His* need. We praise Him because of *our* need. When we praise Him, we're acknowledging that there is only one true God and that He is the Lord over our lives. This enables us to draw upon His strength for victory in every situation we encounter.

Praise lifts us up and out of the troubles of this world and positions us to receive God's presence, peace, power, protection, and provision.

When we praise Him, we're affirming our belief that *HE* is in control of all things!

Once we understand *why* we are to praise God, we need to understand *how* to praise Him.

HOW DO WE PRAISE GOD?

I believe God intends our praise to be dynamic, enthusiastic, and enjoyable! Here are a few Scriptural ways for us to praise the Lord:

SING!

The Bible is filled with verses telling us that singing is a form of praise. Psalm 47:6 is a verse that commands us *four* times to sing! *"Sing praises to God, **sing** praises; **sing** praises to our King, **sing** praises."* We encourage ourselves and others with songs that praise God.

The apostle Paul also tells us to sing: *"Speaking to one another in psalms and hymns and spiritual songs, **singing** and making melody with your heart to the Lord"* (Ephesians 5:19).

You don't have to be an expert vocalist to sing to the Lord. God hears you singing from your heart, not your vocal cords!

SHOUT!

There are more than 30 Biblical references to the people of God shouting their praise. Psalm 98:4-6 says, *"**Shout** joyfully to the LORD, all the earth; break forth and sing for joy and sing praises. Sing praises to the LORD with the lyre, with the lyre and the sound of melody. With trumpets and the sound of the horn **shout** joyfully before the King, the LORD."*

Although shouting to God may sound odd to you, think of it this way: If you're at a sporting event and your team wins the game, what do you do? You shout to celebrate the victory!

Well, since God has won a mighty battle for *us*, we can shout with excitement, joy, and victory to *Him!* Shouting is a joyful, powerful form of praise that both delights God and scares away the enemy!

MAKE MUSIC!

Music is a universal expression of creativity. I believe God created music as a primary means to worship Him and to delight our souls. Although the enemy has tried to appropriate music to advance his own kingdom, Believers around the world continue to use an amazing variety of instruments to praise God.

The focus of Psalm 150 is praise, and it begins with the words, *"Praise the Lord!"* The chapter then goes on to list a variety of instruments used to exalt Him. If you are a musician, use instruments to praise God. He has given you this gift, and when you play for Him, you glorify Him. As you praise God with your musical instrument, both God and you will be blessed.

USE YOUR HANDS!

One of the best "instruments" I can play is my own two hands. *"**Clap** your hands, all peoples; shout to God with the voice of joy"* (Psalm 47:1). Handclapping is a powerful and energizing form of praise.

We also can lift our hands toward Heaven as an expression of praise: *"**Lift up your hands** in the sanctuary and praise the Lord"* (Psalm 134:2). David said in Psalm 63:4, *"I will **lift up my hands** in Your name."*

"Clap your hands, all peoples; shout to God with the voice of joy."

The Hebrew word for "hand" is *yah*. The verb form of this is *yadah*, which means to "praise by lifting the hands." Lifting our hands to the Lord is an outward expression of our inward experience of praise.

DANCE!

Dancing before the Lord is an expression of praise that engages every part of us. The Bible says that when the Spirit of the Lord came upon King David, he *"was **dancing** before the Lord with all his might"* (2 Samuel 6:14).

Just as David's wife Michal despised him for his exuberant expression of praise, there may be some who despise us. But like David, our heart's reply can be, *"I will be more lightly esteemed than this and will be humble in my own eyes"* (v. 22a).

DON'T BE A STONE!

Keep in mind that praising God isn't something reserved only for church. On the contrary, praise is an attitude and a choice we can make regardless of where we are or what we're doing. With God's praises continually in our hearts and on our lips, we will be prepared for times of intimacy with Him.

Be aware, however, that although praise helps prepare the way, it's not a guarantee of intimacy with Him. Sadly, many Believers sing loudly, clap enthusiastically, and may even dance with all their might before Him like King David, but they truly don't *know* the Lord. This is because intimacy with the Lord involves more than singing songs and declaring truths *about* Him.

In Psalm 148, creation itself is commanded to praise the Lord. However, the stars, sun, and moon don't have a relationship with Him. Jesus said that if His disciples held back their praise, then the stones would have to cry out (Luke 19:40). But stones can't be intimate with the Lord.

Don't be a stone! As you praise the Lord with enthusiasm and joy, know that *you* can have an intimate relationship with Him. This is His heart's desire. But know, too, that if you truly want to be intimate with the Lord, there are still three more steps to take on the pathway leading to His presence...

DIGGING DEEPER

1. From childhood until now, what has been your experience in praising the Lord?

2. While most of us are comfortable with using music, song, and clapping to praise Him, many find the thought of shouting, raising our hands, or dancing to express our praise uncomfortable. What forms of praise are you comfortable or uncomfortable with? Why?

3. Are you willing to be bolder in physically expressing your praise to the Lord? Why or why not?

4. Spend time talking to the Lord and praising Him for all He has done, is doing, and will do in your life and in the lives of your loved ones. Ask Him to give you the courage to boldly praise Him in your quiet time alone with Him and in worship with other Believers.

CHAPTER 3

Cross God

OFF YOUR

"To-Do" List

"Come, let us worship and bow down:

let us kneel before the LORD our Maker."

PSALM 95:6

*T*HAT MORNING IN THE COFFEE shop, God told me if I wanted to be intimate with Him, there was a third step I needed to take on the pathway leading into His presence: *"David, after you repent and after you praise Me, I want you to* WORSHIP *Me when you come into My presence."*

I paused to consider exactly what He was saying to me. Some... perhaps even most of us...believe that "praise" and "worship" are synonyms for expressing our adoration to God, but I was learning that isn't accurate. There's a difference between praise and worship:

When I praise God, I am acknowledging what He *does*, but when I worship Him, I am expressing my love for Who He *is*.

While praise CAN lead to worship, this isn't an automatic progression. The sad truth is that I can praise God without ever experiencing true intimacy that comes from worshipping Him.

WAITING ON THE LORD

The Hebrew word used in the Old Testament for "worship" is *shachah*, which means to "stoop, crouch, bow low, fall down flat in an act of submission or reverence before royalty or God." The Greek word for "worship" used predominantly in the New Testament is *proskuneo*, which is a combination of two words: *pros* (toward) + *kuneo* (to kiss). It means "to kiss, like a dog licking its master's hand, to prostrate, bow down, show reverence for, adore."

When I worship the Lord, I submit myself to Him. I bow before Him in absolute humility. I "kiss" Him with my spirit. I honor the One to Whom all honor is due.

As I worship the Lord, I commune with Him at the deepest level of my spirit, where *"deep calls to deep"* (Psalm 42:7). In this place of intimacy, I hold nothing back from Him. I invite Him to "into me see." I experience His love for me, and He experiences my love for Him. This is only possible because true worship is a place of absolute trust. I'm not afraid of what God will say or do or expect of me in these moments of vulnerability.

A vital aspect of worship is *waiting* on the Lord. We are told 38 times in the Old Testament to wait on Him. What does this mean?

The Hebrew word for "wait" is *yachal:* "to wait, tarry, hope, expect, anticipate."

In Psalm 27:14, David exhorts us, *"**Wait** for the LORD; be strong and let your heart take courage; yes, **wait** for the LORD."*

The prophet Micah vowed, *"But as for me, I will watch expectantly for the LORD; I will **wait** for the God of my salvation. My God will hear me"* (Micah 7:7).

When we're seeking times of intimacy with God...when we have repented for our sins and praised Him...when we have moved into that place of worship and expressing our love and adoration for Him...it's because we desperately want to experience a sense of His love for us. But the truth is that in our limited humanity, we don't always experience His presence and sense Him right here with us.

Many times, God's presence in worship only comes as we wait in hope-filled expectation and anticipation, believing that as much as we want to be with Him, He wants to be with us even more. Too often we rush into our quiet times with the Lord as though He is an item needing to be accomplished and checked off on our "to-do list" after 15 minutes.

We're all too easily content with a devotional reading, a verse or two of Scripture, and then a simple prayer in which we express our thanksgiving and praise. We seldom *wait* before the Lord in true worship. God loves it when we linger with Him, and even seems to deliberately pause to make sure we truly desire to be *with* Him before blessing us with an overwhelming awareness of His presence.

In Acts 1:4, Jesus told His disciples to remain in Jerusalem and *"wait for what the Father had promised."* We also know from 1 Corinthians 15:6 that Jesus had appeared to 500 of His followers after His resurrection from the dead.

Do you know that of these 500, only *120* disciples were in the upper room on the Day of Pentecost, fellowshipping together, praying, and waiting on the Lord? Only 120 tarried. Only 120 were changed because they waited. Only 120 experienced a powerful outpouring of His presence...*a mere 25%.*

The other 380 followers chose to do something else that day, and by making that choice, they missed out on an indescribable blessing. Wouldn't it have been terrible to be one of the disciples who got tired of waiting and just went on home because we were busy or bored?

*"Wait for the LORD; be strong and let your heart take courage; yes, **wait** for the LORD."*

WAITING IN THE MIDST OF SUFFERING

Sometimes we may feel as though it's simply too hard to wait on the Lord, especially when we're in the midst of painful circumstances. We may grow impatient with God, believing that if He only knew how much we were suffering, He wouldn't make us wait for His presence to come and comfort us.

But the reality is that God's presence doesn't manifest because we're suffering. His presence comes in response to our *brokenness*. When we're broken, the Heavens open:

"The righteous cry, and the LORD hears and delivers them out of all their troubles. The LORD is near to the brokenhearted and saves those who are crushed in spirit. Many are the afflictions of the righteous, but the LORD delivers him out of them all" (Psalm 34:17-19).

As we wait on the Lord day by day in worshipful, hope-filled expectation, He comes and ministers His comfort and strength, healing and hope to us. Never underestimate the power of time spent in God's presence. In a single moment, we can be healed and our circumstances changed. Jacob had an encounter in God's presence, and in a moment...

- His name was changed.
- His walk was changed.
- His entire destiny was changed!

There's a wonderful chorus I love to sing called, "In the presence of Jehovah":

In the presence of Jehovah
God Almighty, Prince of Peace
Troubles vanish, hearts are mended
In the presence of the King.

–GERON AND BECKY DAVIS

My friend, there are things you simply can't find in the Lord's presence: sin...sickness...doubt...worry...guilt...fear...depression... loneliness...heartache. All of these must disappear when confronted with God's power and love. As you faithfully wait on Him in worship, you will discover that *anything* can happen in the presence of the King!

Does spending time with God sometimes feel like a burden, a religious obligation, or a chore? If so, cross Him off your "to-do" list forever! Be willing to *WAIT* on Him, trusting that He simply wants to *be* with you and bless you with His amazing love.

I invite you to enter into the intimacy of true worship before the Lord. I promise you won't regret taking this vital, life-changing step on your journey into the heart of God.

DIGGING DEEPER

1. The primary difference between praise and worship is that when we praise God, we're acknowledging what He *does*, and when we worship Him, we're expressing our love for Who He *is*. Describe the difference between praise and worship as you have experienced them in your life.

2. Is it easy or difficult for you to openly express your love for the Lord? Why?

3. The meaning for "worship" in the original Greek used in the New Testament means to "kiss, like a dog licking its master's hand, to prostrate, bow down, show reverence for, adore." Are you comfortable with this definition? Why or why not?

4. Spend time with the Lord in worship. As you humble yourself before Him and express your love, be willing to wait on Him, knowing that *anything* can happen in God's presence.

CHAPTER 4

He Wants It ALL

"And my God will supply all your needs according to

His riches in glory in Christ Jesus."

PHILIPPIANS 4:19

*A*s I sat sipping my coffee and pondering what the Lord was saying to me about repentance, praise, and worship, He gave me yet another step to take on the pathway into His presence: **"OFFERING."**

He said, *"David, after you have repented, after you have praised Me, after you have entered into true worship, know that My requirements for intimacy also include bringing me an **OFFERING.**"*

Since Barbara and I always tithe faithfully, when God told me that bringing Him an **"OFFERING"** was one of the five steps to intimacy with Him, I paid attention. I realized He was talking about more than giving Him 10% of my weekly paycheck.

When church folks hear the word "offering," we usually begin looking around for the ushers and the offering plate. And faithfully giving our financial gifts to the Lord *is* a vital step on our journey toward intimacy. Why? Because our level of giving reflects our level of trust in God and our belief in His desire and ability to provide for our every need. When we give Him our tithes and special offerings, we're demonstrating our trust in His promise to abundantly bless our obedience and rebuke the devourer for our sake:

"*'Bring the whole tithe into the storehouse, so that there may be food in My house, and test Me now in this,' says the LORD of hosts, 'if I will not open for you the windows of heaven and pour out for you a blessing until it overflows.*

"*'Then I will rebuke the devourer for you, so that it will not destroy the fruits of the ground; nor will your vine in the field cast its grapes,' says the LORD of hosts. 'All the nations will call you blessed, for you shall be a delightful land,' says the LORD of hosts*" (Malachi 3:10-12).

So yes, consistently giving back to God a portion of what He has given to us is vital to experiencing intimacy with Him.

But when He told me that I needed to bring Him an offering in my intimate times with Him, He was requiring more of me than my wallet. You see, *nothing* I have is mine.

"All the nations will call you blessed, for you shall be a delightful land," says the LORD of hosts."

MINE!

As the parents of two children and the grandparents of five, Barbara and I are well acquainted with a two-year-old's tendency to grab a favorite toy and clutch it tightly while loudly declaring, "MINE!" Attempts to remove the coveted object typically result in loud objections accompanied by dramatic sobs.

A lot of Believers are the same way. Somewhere along the way we got the mistaken notion that whatever is within our grasp belongs to us. My friend, this simply isn't so. *Everything* we own is in our possession ONLY because God has given it to us or allowed us to have it. *Nothing* belongs to us, as King David declared:

*"**Yours,** O LORD, is the greatness and the power and the glory and the victory and the majesty, indeed everything that is in the heavens and the earth; **Yours** is the dominion, O LORD, and You exalt Yourself as head over all.*

"Both riches and honor come from You, and You rule over all, and in Your hand is power and might; and it lies in Your hand to make great and to strengthen everyone" (1 Chronicles 29:11-12).

This means that every material belonging...clothes, cars, furniture, houses, books, computers, checkbooks, credit cards...it *ALL* belongs to Him. And although we may cry out, "MINE!" when something we think we own is threatened, the truth is, it's *HIS!* The Lord calls us to love Him more than all our worldly goods.

The same is true of our time and talents. Neither belongs to us. As with our treasure, our time, skills, and spiritual gifts are God's to be used at His discretion. When we are moving into intimacy with Him, we will clearly hear Him tell us when and where and how to use these resources that He has so lovingly and generously given us.

It's easy to be afraid that if we let go of the little bit of treasure, time, or talents we have, there won't be enough left over for us. But this simply isn't true. In God's economy, when we let go of what we have as a demonstration of worship and obedience to Him, He multiplies our offerings back to us in the form of His blessings in our lives.

ALL!

Many of us are very familiar with this comforting passage from Philippians 4:19: *"And my God will supply **all** your needs according to His riches in glory in Christ Jesus."* But many of us are unfamiliar with the verse that precedes it:

"But I have received everything in full and have an abundance; I am amply supplied, having received from Epaphroditus what you have sent, a fragrant aroma, an acceptable sacrifice, well-pleasing to God" (v.18).

The relationship between these two verses is pretty subtle, so it can be easy to miss. In verse 18, Paul tells the folks in the church at

Philippi that he has received the sacrificial gift they had sent to him, and in the next verse he tells them that because *they* have supplied *Paul's* needs, *God* would supply *their* needs (v. 19).

Do you see the correlation? The Philippian Believers must have had an intimate relationship with the Lord based on trust, because they were willing to give generously to take care of His servant. And Paul assured them that this trust was not unfounded, because God would supply *ALL* their needs. How much is "all"?*ALL!*

Paul also wrote to the Corinthian church about giving generous offerings and then trusting God to supply all their needs:

"Each one must do just as he has purposed in his heart, not grudgingly or under compulsion, for God loves a cheerful giver. And God is able to make all grace abound to you, so that always having all sufficiency in everything, you may have an abundance for every good deed" (2 Corinthians 9: 8-9).

What did Paul say would happen if the Corinthians cheerfully worshipped God with their offerings? He would make *ALL* grace abound to them, and they would have *ALL* sufficiency in everything they needed. How much is "all"? *ALL!*

If we desire intimacy with the Lord, we must acknowledge that *ALL* we have and *ALL* we are is His. And if He should require any of our time, talent, or treasure, we must willingly relinquish anything and everything to Him and then trust Him to supply *ALL* our needs.

My friend, don't be afraid to worship the Lord with your offerings. Choose to trust Him with everything you are and everything you have. As you do, you will experience increasingly deeper levels of intimacy with the One who loves you so.

DIGGING DEEPER

1. What has been your life experience with tithing and giving God special offerings? Are you trusting in His promise in Malachi 3:10-12 to bless your giving and rebuke the devourer in response to your faithful giving? Why or why not?

2. Is there anything you are calling, **"MINE!"** and withholding from the Lord?

3. Are you willing now for Him to have *ALL* that you have and *ALL* that you are? Why or why not? Be honest with yourself and with Him.

4. Spend time with the Lord asking Him to reveal anything you are clutching to yourself. Agree with Him that according to 1 Chronicles 29:11-12, everything you have belongs to Him. Ask Him to help you release *ALL* things into His care and to help you trust Him to supply *ALL* of your needs because of His great love for you.

CHAPTER 5

Burnt Flesh

"I urge you, brethren, by the mercies of God,

to present your bodies a living and holy sacrifice, acceptable to

God, which is your spiritual service of worship."

ROMANS 12:1

*T*HE FIFTH AND FINAL WORD God spoke to me that morning in the hotel coffee shop was *"SACRIFICE."* Now there's a word that could make a person nervous! But because I trust in God's amazing love for me, I knew He wasn't asking anything of me I wasn't able to give Him.

"Lord," I asked, "what do you mean? What kind of sacrifice do You want me to bring You?"

He replied, *"David, you can't bring Me an offering without sacrifice."*

I thought of the story in 2 Samuel 24 when King David wanted to build an altar to the Lord, and although Araunah freely offered to give him all the items he needed for the sacrifice, he insisted on paying for the supplies, declaring, *"I will not offer burnt offerings to the LORD my God which cost me nothing"* (v. 24).

David knew he needed to pay a price for his offering. He realized his gift required a sacrifice on his part if it was to be meaningful both to him *and* to God.

What was true for King David then is still true for us today. God doesn't want our token offerings that basically cost us nothing...the $10 check in the offering plate that doesn't impact our trip to the mall...begrudgingly serving someone in need...a quick 10-minute devotional reading squeezed into our morning routine just so we can say we spent time with Him.

God doesn't want our second best, and He isn't interested in the crumbs from our table. No, God was telling me that morning that if I want to be intimate with Him, then I must be willing to make *sacrifices* for Him. The gifts of my time, talent, and treasure have to truly cost me something. If our gifts are precious to us, they will be precious to God as well.

When God asked Abraham if he was willing to sacrifice his only son Isaac, He was testing Abraham to see if he was willing to offer God the most precious thing in the world to him: the promise for which Abraham and Sarah had waited for 27 years. And Abraham demonstrated with his obedience that he was willing:

"By Myself I have sworn,' declares the LORD, 'because you have done this thing and have not withheld your son, your only son, indeed I will greatly bless you, and I will greatly multiply your seed as the stars of the heavens and as the sand which is on the seashore; and your seed shall possess the gate of their enemies. In your seed all the nations of the earth shall be blessed, because you have obeyed My voice'" (Genesis 22:16-18).

Because Abraham withheld *nothing* from God. He blessed him by confirming and then fulfilling the covenant He had made with him years before, so that his offspring *did* become as the *"stars in the heavens"* and the *"sand which is on the seashore"!*

Likewise, I believe the Lord was asking something else of me that morning. I sensed He was asking me if I would be willing to offer my very *life* as a living sacrifice to Him.

LIVING SACRIFICES

You know, the painful truth is that I could...

- Repent every day
- Praise God with enthusiasm
- Worship Him passionately
- Offer Him *all* of my time, treasure, and talent
- Give Him the most precious thing in the world to me...

...but there still would be *one* thing preventing me from walking in a deeply intimate relationship with the Lord:

ME.

Just like a wife who willingly cooks the meals, cleans the house, and meets all of her husband's physical needs but withholds the deepest part of her heart and soul from him, so we, too, can serve the Lord faithfully without ever being truly intimate with Him.

You see, intimacy with the Lord means giving myself to Him with *abandon.* I could do everything He told me to do and give Him everything He asked me to give, but if I withhold myself from Him, I will never experience true intimacy with the Lord.

In his letter to the Roman Christians, Paul wrote, *"I urge you, brethren, by the mercies of God, to present your bodies a living and holy sacrifice, acceptable to God, which is your spiritual service of worship. And do not be conformed to this world, but be transformed by the renewing of your mind, so that you may prove what the will of God is, that which is good and acceptable and perfect"* (Romans 12:1).

Most of us think that the word "sacrifice" means to give up something. In Hebrew, the word sacrifice is *korban.* It means "to draw near to." The goal of the Tabernacle sacrifices was to draw God's people near to Him. This is what God wants you and me to do.

So many of us spend our lives hopping on and off God's altar. Our hearts can be stirred with passion, and so we give ourselves to Him as a living sacrifice, we draw near to Him for a day, a week, a month and then we have better things to do. Like Peter, we vow that we're willing to go with the Lord even to death (Luke 22:33). But then when the fire gets too painful or it seems as though God's requirements are too hard, instead of pressing further into Him, we jump off and run away with our flesh only half burnt away. And the truth is that burnt flesh smells pretty bad!

To continue on this pathway into the intimacy of God's presence, we must choose to climb up on His altar and offer ourselves—body, soul, and spirit—as a living sacrifice, to draw near to Him and allow His bonds of love to hold us in place until every part of our flesh that does not bring Him glory is consumed.

Then like Paul, we can say, *"I have been crucified with Christ; and it is no longer I who live, but Christ lives in me; and the life which I now live in the flesh I live by faith in the Son of God, who loved me and gave Himself up for me"* (Galatians 2:20).

THE CRY OF THE DESPERATE

In Mark 10 we read the story of a blind man who was desperate for an encounter with Jesus. Bartimaeus spent his days sitting by the side of the road, begging for food, money...anything that could temporarily alleviate the painful circumstances of his life.

But then one day, he heard Jesus and His disciples passing by: *"When he heard that it was Jesus the Nazarene, he began to cry out and say, 'Jesus, Son of David, have mercy on me!'"* (v. 47)

It appeared that Jesus was going to just walk on by the blind beggar, but in response to those who tried to silence his cries, Bartimaeus simply cried out all the more, "Son of David, have mercy on me!" (v. 48)

Bartimaeus knew that one encounter with Jesus could impact His life forever. He was a desperate man who was desperate for change, and so he was not ashamed to cry out to Jesus. He persistently refused to be silenced or embarrassed by the opinions of others, and his persistence was honored when Jesus responded to his cries and healed his blindness.

My friend, are *you* desperate for an encounter with the Lord? Do you have a hunger for intimacy with Him that cannot be satisfied any other way? Are you willing to take these five steps that will lead you on the pathway to His presence? Will you cry out for His touch as you...

- Repent before Him?
- Praise Him wholeheartedly?
- Worship Him passionately?
- Offer Him your time, treasure, and talents?
- Remain a living sacrifice on His altar?

If so, then come with me now as we continue on this journey....

DIGGING DEEPER

1. Think about the offerings you have given to the Lord in recent months. Have they been your second best or have they truly cost you something?

2. How does it make you feel to know that God is calling you to be a "living sacrifice" for Him?

3. Have you given yourself to the Lord with abandon? Why or why not?

4. Spend time with God now repenting for any sin, praising Him, worshipping Him, and offering Him your all. Ask Him for His courage, grace, and strength to be a living sacrifice for Him to His glory.

PART II

The Journey Begins

CHAPTER 6

Pictures, Patterns, and Mysteries

"You will seek Me and find Me

when you search for Me with all your heart."

JEREMIAH 29:13

*W*HEN YOU WERE A KID, did you ever
pretend to be a pirate and make a map where an X marked the spot to
treasure buried in your back yard?

Well, the Word of God is like a treasure map, except the treasure
contained in Scripture isn't pretend...it's pure gold! Just as a treasure
map leads to buried riches, when we diligently follow the map of the
Bible, we discover the amazing riches He's buried there for us to find.
But we must *dig* for them.

As I've been studying the Bible over the years, God has been
revealing mysteries to me that have profoundly impacted me on my
journey toward intimacy with Him. Now let me assure you, He hasn't
been showing me these secrets because I'm someone special. God
has been sharing deep truths with me because I've asked Him, I've
pursued Him, and because I've waited and listened for His answers.
My friend, He wants to share His mysteries with you, too.

King Solomon observed, *"It is the glory of God to conceal a matter,
but the glory of kings is to search out a matter"* (Proverbs 25:2).

Most times, the deep things of God are not clearly understood
by our natural minds. He only begins to reveal the hidden treasures

of His Word as we passionately search for Him, driven by a desperate hunger to truly know Him and His ways. When we dig for God's gold buried within Scripture, He assures us, *"You will seek Me and find Me when you search for Me with all your heart"* (Jeremiah 29:13).

"You will seek Me and find Me when you search for Me with all your heart."

As I sought God and asked Him to reveal Himself to me through His Word, He reminded me of His promise in James 4:8: *"Draw near to God, and He will draw near to you."* And so I began to draw near to Him in ways I never had before, and as I did, He started revealing to me the pictures and patterns hidden in His Word.

PAINTED PICTURES

When I was a little boy, my parents faithfully took me to Sunday school. I loved the big Bible in the children's department because it was full of pictures. I would slowly turn the pages, captivated by the illustrations of Noah and the ark, Moses parting the Red Sea, and Daniel in the lion's den.

The Bible is full of pictures. But as adults, we often just read the words written on the pages while failing to see the amazing pictures God has painted for us in His Word.

He has included these pictures because He is trying to teach us a vital truth about how He communicates with His children:

God uses the *natural* world to reveal deep *spiritual* truths to us.

Jesus frequently used the natural to reveal the spiritual by teaching His followers in parables— earthly stories with heavenly meanings. He revealed truths about God's Kingdom through a seed, a pearl, and a fishnet (Matthew 14). He used a flock of sheep and a shepherd to teach how His disciples are to follow Him and listen for His voice (John 10). He pointed to a grapevine and its branches to demonstrate our need to abide in Him if we want to bear good fruit for eternity (John 15).

When the disciples came to Jesus and asked why He taught in parables, He replied, *"To you it has been granted to know the mysteries of the kingdom of heaven, but to them it has not been granted"* (Matthew 13:11).

The mysteries of Heaven are like treasures of gold imbedded deep in God's Word that must be mined if they are to be discovered, understood, and applied to our lives.

THE NATURAL AND THE SPIRITUAL

In his letter to the Roman Christians, Paul said, *"For the invisible things of Him from the creation of the world are clearly seen, being understood by the things that are made, even His eternal power and Godhead; so that they are without excuse"* (Romans 1:20).

Paul was saying that God has used what is visible to teach about what is invisible. He emphasizes this again in his letter to the Believers in Corinth: *"So also it is written, 'The first man, Adam, became a living soul.' The last Adam became a life-giving spirit. However, the spiritual is not first, but the natural; then the spiritual"* (1 Corinthians 15:45-46).

Let me say it again: God uses the *natural* to reveal the *spiritual.* He uses pictures and patterns to teach us eternal truths.

When I cried out to God that I hungered to know Him more intimately, I was amazed as He began revealing to me the mysteries of the patterns hidden in the Tabernacle and the Temple. Why was He teaching me about the Israelites' holy places of worship, when what I had asked for was a deeper, more intimate relationship with Him?

Because hidden in the patterns of the Tabernacle and the Temple is the pathway to His presence! And the more He has revealed to me about this pattern, the more intimate my relationship with Him has grown.

'SHOW THE HOUSE TO THE HOUSE'

In my introduction I mentioned that I was reading Ezekiel 43 one day and came across something that almost knocked me off my chair. God tells Ezekiel:

*"Thou son of man, **show the house to the house** of Israel, that they may be ashamed of their iniquities: and let them measure the pattern. And if they be ashamed of all that they have done, show them the form of the house...and write it in their sight, that they may keep the whole form thereof, and all the ordinances thereof, and do them"* (vs. 10-11 KJV).

God said, *"Show the house to the house."* What was the first *"house"* to which God was referring? The Temple! And who is the second *"house"*? The children of Israel! Why was Ezekiel to *"show the house to the house"*? So that the Israelites could understand the revelations of the pattern of the Temple and be ashamed of their sin!

God was telling Ezekiel, *"I've given you the pattern of My Temple to follow. Now I want you to tell My people to look at this pattern, measure the pattern, and compare themselves to the pattern, so that they can be convicted of their sin and return to Me."*

After reading this passage, I had a fresh revelation that the Temple wasn't just a house of worship thousands of years ago in Old Testament times. The picture God painted for us in Scripture of the Temple is for you and me *today*. There is a life-giving, life-changing, eternity-impacting purpose to its pattern.

You see, what happened under the Old Covenant was a blueprint for the New Covenant, and together, the Old and New Covenants form a blueprint for us today. Paul tells us that the things that happened to the children of Israel were to teach *them* AND to teach *us:*

"Now these things happened to them as an example, and they were written for our instruction, upon whom the ends of the ages have come. Therefore let him who thinks he stands take heed that he does not fall" (1 Corinthians 10:11-12).

Remember...God uses the *natural* to reveal the *spiritual*.

GOD'S HEAVENLY TABERNACLE

Even though I had grown up as a preacher's kid and had read the Word over and over again, I had no idea there was a Tabernacle in Heaven. But one day, God showed me that there is, in fact, a holy Tabernacle in the Heavenly realm...the very one that provided the pattern for the Israelites' earthly Tabernacle in the wilderness!

The writer of Hebrews says, *"...just as Moses was warned by God when he was about to erect the tabernacle; for, 'See,' He says, 'that you make all things according to the pattern which was shown you on the mountain'"* (8:5).

According to Scripture, God took Moses to the top of a mountain and showed him a pattern for how to build the Tabernacle. Well, to what mountain did God take him? It couldn't have been Mount Sinai, because there wasn't a Tabernacle on Mount Sinai for Moses to see.

So where was the mountain where God showed Moses the pattern? I believe that God took Moses to Mount Zion in a vision, showed him the Temple in Heaven, and then said, *"Let them construct a sanctuary for Me, that I may dwell among them. According to all that I am going to show you, as the pattern of the tabernacle and the pattern of all its furniture, just so you shall construct it"* (Exodus 25:8-9)!

Hebrews 9:23-24 also refers to the pattern (or the *"copies"*) of Heaven:

"Therefore it was necessary for the copies of the things in the heavens to be cleansed with these, but the heavenly things themselves with better sacrifices than these. For Christ did not enter a holy place made with hands, a mere copy of the true one, but into heaven itself, now to appear in the presence of God for us."

In Exodus 25-31, we read about the intricate plans for the Tabernacle that God revealed to Moses, including the funding, the building, the furniture, the coverings, the priests, and the sacrifices... details that even included the pegs on which the serving utensils were to hang! Every item had meaning.

Moses was with God for 40 days observing and learning about

the pattern, and when God had revealed all the details to him that he needed to complete the task, He sent Moses back to build the Tabernacle according to the exact instructions he had been given.

(Note: To clarify, the *wilderness Tabernacle*, constructed according to the plan God revealed to Moses on Mt. Sinai, was God's temporary dwelling place and the Israelites' house of worship during their exodus from Egypt.

The *Jerusalem Temple* was commissioned by Solomon, King David's son, to be the Israelites' "permanent" house of worship. However, it was destroyed by the Romans in 70 AD, and all that remains is a portion of a wall, known today as the Wailing Wall. I'll share more with you about the Temple in the next chapter.)

MOSES AND JESUS

When Jesus was confronted by religious Jews because He performed miracles on the Sabbath and claimed that God was His Father, He gave an amazing response to their accusations:

*"Do not think that I will accuse you before the Father; the one who accuses you is Moses, in whom you have set your hope. **For if you believed Moses, you would believe Me, for he wrote about Me.** But if you do not believe his writings, how will you believe My words?"* (John 5:45-47).

Wait a second...*Moses* wrote about *Jesus?*

Moses wrote the first five books of the Old Covenant known as the Torah: Genesis, Exodus, Leviticus, Numbers, and Deuteronomy. I have read these books and re-read them and re-re-read them, and I can assure you: The name of Jesus is not mentioned once.

So why did Jesus say, *"For if you believed Moses, you would believe Me, for he wrote about Me"*? Because Jesus is revealed in the pattern of the Tabernacle!

When God showed Moses the pattern for building the Tabernacle, there was significance far beyond building a house of worship for God's people as they wandered in the wilderness. God was revealing

God was revealing a

picture...a pattern...a plan...

and a purpose for

how all future generations

could have an intimate

relationship with Him.

a picture...a pattern...a plan...and a purpose for how all future generations could have an intimate relationship with Him.

YOU ARE THE TEMPLE

The pictures and pattern of the wilderness Tabernacle and Solomon's Temple have tremendous impact for you and me today. The pictures God painted in His Word and the patterns He ordained thousands of years ago apply to *you* and me NOW.

Paul wrote, *"Do you not know that your body is a temple of the Holy Spirit who is in you, whom you have from God, and that you are not your own? For you have been bought with a price: therefore glorify God in your body"* (1 Corinthians 6:19-20).

We don't belong to ourselves. We are God's, and He has a holy purpose for each of our lives. And not only are we the living Tabernacle of God in which He now dwells, but we also are priests serving the Most High God:

"But you are a chosen race, a royal priesthood, a holy nation, a people for God's own possession, so that you may proclaim the excellencies of Him who has called you out of darkness into His marvelous light" (1 Peter 2:9).

God wants *all* of His children to know Him and to search out His ways. The goal of this book is to share with you the mysteries God has revealed to me throughout the last several years...mysteries that will help draw you into a more intimate relationship with Him.

As you continue on your journey toward intimacy with the Lord, I encourage you to dig deep into His Word to discover the rich storehouse of treasure He has laid up for you, both in this life now and for all eternity.

DIGGING DEEPER

1. God uses the *natural* to *reveal* the spiritual. Think of an example in your own life when He has used something in the natural world to teach you a spiritual truth.

2. James 4:8 promises, *"Draw near to God, and He will draw near to you."* How near do you feel to God today? On a scale of 1 to 10, with 1 being completely alienated from God and 10 being enveloped by His loving presence, where would you place yourself?

3. Are you living *"as though you are not your own"* and as though *"your body is a temple of the Holy Spirit"*? Why or why not?

4. Spend time now talking with the Lord about your hunger—or lack of hunger—for a more intimate relationship with Him. Ask Him to stir up a desire in you to dig deeper into His Word to discover the "gold" He has buried there for you.

CHAPTER 7

Fire and Glory

"The house that is to be built for the LORD

shall be exceedingly magnificent,

famous and glorious throughout all lands."

1 CHRONICLES 22:5

*W*HEN I CRIED OUT TO GOD that I wanted to truly know Him, He gave me the five steps I shared in Part 1 of this book: **REPENT, PRAISE, WORSHIP, OFFERING,** and **SACRIFICE.**

But His revelation didn't stop there. In fact, little did I know that what God had spoken to my spirit that morning in the hotel was only the beginning of the mysteries He wanted to reveal to me, mysteries that up until then had been veiled from my spiritual eyes and ears.

Throughout the next several years, God surprised me with rich treasures buried in His Word...treasures of pictures and patterns hidden in the Old Testament about the wilderness Tabernacle and Solomon's Temple.

'ARISE, THEREFORE, AND BUILD'

As you may know, Solomon's Temple was built following the pattern of Moses' Tabernacle in the wilderness.

Even though King David knew he was not the one chosen to build the Temple (2 Samuel 7), he still was passionate about the construction of God's house of worship in Jerusalem.

He said, ***"The house that is to be built for the LORD shall be*** *exceedingly magnificent, famous and glorious throughout all lands. Therefore now I will make preparation for it"* (1 Chronicles 22:5).

Knowing that God had ordained his son Solomon to be crowned king after him, David was diligent to provide the resources needed to accomplish this monumental task. When David commissioned Solomon with the task of building the Temple, he listed the provisions he had made ready for his son:

- 100,000 talents of gold
- 1,000,000 talents of silver
- Bronze and iron *"beyond weight"*
- Timber and stone
- Workmen, stonecutters, masons, carpenters, and skilled men

As a loving father, King David sternly admonished his son to remain faithful to the Lord in the construction process and throughout his reign:

"Only the LORD give you discretion and understanding, and give you charge over Israel, so that you may keep the law of the LORD your God. Then you will prosper, if you are careful to observe the statutes and the ordinances which the LORD commanded Moses concerning Israel. Be strong and courageous, do not fear nor be dismayed" (vs. 12-13).

As a student of the Israelites' history and God's Law, David knew that the blessings of God's presence, power, peace, protection, and prosperity were available only to those who walked in an obedient, faith-filled Covenant Relationship with Him. He also knew that, conversely, those who walked in disobedience and rebellion would receive God's judgment and the withdrawal of His Covenant Blessings.

Then David commanded Solomon, *"Now set your heart and your soul to seek the LORD your God; arise, therefore, and build the sanctuary of the LORD God, so that you may bring the ark of the covenant of the LORD and the holy vessels of God into the house that is to be built for the name of the LORD"* (v. 19).

In the fourth year of his reign in about 960 B.C., King Solomon began building the Temple on Mt. Moriah in Jerusalem, and the construction continued for seven years until it was finally completed around 953 B.C. The site where Solomon chose to establish the Temple was a place of tremendous historic significance to the Israelites.

The area of Mount Moriah is where Abraham encountered the high priest Melchizedek (Genesis 14) and honored him by paying the first tithe recorded in Scripture. Years later, Abraham's faith was severely tested when he obeyed God by returning to Mt. Moriah with Isaac to offer his long-awaited promised son to the Lord as a sacrifice (Genesis 22).

It was on Mt. Moriah 900 years later when David repented for a serious sin by buying Araunah's threshing-room floor, building an altar on it, and offering God a sacrifice (1 Chronicles 21; 2 Samuel 24). Some historians also believe that it was near Mt. Moriah that Jesus was crucified, which would serve as the prophetic fulfillment of Abraham's words to his son: *"God will provide for Himself the lamb"* (Genesis 22:8).

Mt. Moriah clearly was a place that spoke to the Jewish people of sacrifice, and it was here that Solomon built this center of sacrifice and worship to the Most High God.

"Now set your heart and your soul to seek the LORD your God; arise, therefore, and build the sanctuary of the LORD God..."

'EXCEEDINGLY MAGNIFICENT'

When the Temple was completed, Solomon had all the furniture and articles that had been carefully designed and built put into place:

"Thus all the work that Solomon performed for the house of the LORD was finished. And Solomon brought in the things that David his father had dedicated, even the silver and the gold and all the utensils, and put them in the treasuries of the house of God" (2 Chronicles 5:1).

Once this was done, the most amazing worship service ever celebrated on earth began. So many sheep and oxen were sacrificed that they *"could not be counted or numbered"* (v. 6). Then the priests and the Levites brought up the Ark of the Covenant from the temporary tent King David had erected and placed the Ark in the Holy of Holies.

After the priests came out of the Most Holy Place, they began playing cymbals, stringed instruments, harps, trumpets, and other instruments of music while all the Levites glorified the Lord and praised Him with thanksgiving, singing in unison: *"He indeed is good for His lovingkindness is everlasting."*

As the glorious sound of music and singing washed over all of Jerusalem, God responded to their worship with His manifested presence: *"Then the house, the house of the LORD, was filled with a cloud, so that the priests could not stand to minister because of the cloud, for the glory of the LORD filled the house of God"* (v. 13-14).

Solomon then fell to his knees and prayed a passionate prayer dedicating the Temple to God, and concluded with this plea:

"Now therefore arise, O LORD God, to Your resting place, You and the ark of Your might; let Your priests, O LORD God, be clothed with salvation and let Your godly ones rejoice in what is good. O LORD God, do not turn away the face of Your anointed; remember Your lovingkindness to Your servant David" (6:41-42).

When Solomon finished praying, fire came down from Heaven and consumed their sacrifices and offerings, and the glory of the Lord filled the Temple to such a degree that the priests could not even enter the building! In response to the fire and the glory, the Israelites fell on their faces before the Lord in worship.

This moment was the fulfillment of King David's heart's desire: Truly the Temple was an *"exceedingly magnificent, famous, and glorious"* house of worship to the Most High God.

You would think that after such a glorious, power-filled, life-changing experience, Solomon would have followed in his father's footsteps as a faithful worshipper of God all the days of his life. But sadly, this wasn't the case.

1 Kings 11 tells the tragic story of how the wisest man who ever lived became the greatest of fools:

"Solomon did what was evil in the sight of the LORD, and did not follow the LORD fully, as David his father had done. Then Solomon built a high place for Chemosh the detestable idol of Moab, on the mountain which is east of Jerusalem, and for Molech the detestable idol of the sons of Ammon.

"Thus also he did for all his foreign wives, who burned incense and sacrificed to their gods. Now the LORD was angry with Solomon because his heart was turned away from the LORD, the God of Israel, who had appeared to him twice, and had commanded him concerning this thing, that he should not go after other gods; but he did not observe what the LORD had commanded" (vs. 6-10).

What follows is the beginning of the end of Solomon's reign. Rather than the glory and the fire being preserved and maintained in the Temple throughout the generations of the Israelites, the rebellion of Solomon spilled on to God's chosen people and eventually resulted in the Temple's destruction by King Nebuchadnezzar's Babylonian army less than 400 years later.

However, the details of this glorious house of worship for the Most High God have been preserved forever in His Word, first in the explicit directions He gave to Moses for the construction of the wilderness Tabernacle (Exodus 26-31; 37-40), and then later in the detailed outline for the building of the Temple (1 Kings 6-8; 2 Chronicles 2-7).

Next I want to share with you the details of the pictures and patterns hidden in Scripture, so that you, too, may have an increasingly intimate relationship with the Lord.

Join me as we continue our journey on the pathway into God's presence...

DIGGING DEEPER

1. Consider the most powerful times of worship you've ever experienced. How do they compare to the worship service when Solomon dedicated the Temple to the Lord?

2. The blessings of God's presence, power, peace, protection, and prosperity are available to all those who choose to walk in an obedient, faith-filled Covenant Relationship with Him. Does this describe your relationship with God?

3. In what areas of your life do you need to know and experience more of His presence, power, peace, protection, and prosperity?

4. Spend time with the Lord asking Him to show you anything that may be blocking you from receiving His blessings. If He reveals any sin or doubt, confess it and then ask for His courage, strength, and grace to walk intimately with Him in Covenant Relationship.

CHAPTER 8

The Beginning
OF THE *Pattern*

"Now these things happened to them

as an example, and they

were written for our instruction."

1 CORINTHIANS 10:11

*A*S CHILDREN, MANY OF US learned the Sunday school stories of the Exodus. We were taught how God sent Moses to Pharaoh to demand, "Let my people go," how God hardened Pharaoh's heart. How God sent 10 plagues against the people and land of Egypt until finally Pharaoh relented and allowed the Israelite people to leave, but there's much more to the story...

Exodus 9:16 tells us why God hardened Pharaoh's heart: *"For this reason I have allowed you to remain in order to show you My power, and in order to proclaim My name though all the earth."* And again in Exodus 10:1-2: *"Go to Pharaoh, for I have hardened his heart and the heart of his servants, that I may perform these signs of Mine among them, and that you may tell in the hearing of your son, and of your grandson, how I made a mockery of the Egyptians, and how I performed My signs among them; that you may know that I am the LORD."*

Even while God was making a name for Himself, He was making a mockery of the Egyptians as a spiritual representation of the world. Did you know that the Bible describes how literally hundreds of years after Israel left Egypt, the nations Israel came in contact with had heard how God had delivered His people from the hand of the Egyptians?

GOD IS SUPREME

Why 10 plagues? What's the mystery and significance? There were at least 10 different gods the Egyptians revered and worshipped.

1. When God used Moses to turn the water into blood, He was demonstrating to the Egyptians that He was greater than Hapi, their god of the Nile.

2. When God brought the plague of frogs to overtake the land He was demonstrating to the Egyptians that He was greater than Heqt, their god of the frogs.

3. When God caused lice to swarm the banks of the Nile and infect the Egyptian people, He was demonstrating to the Egyptians that He was greater than Kheper, their insect god.

4. When God brought the plague of flies to cover the land, He was demonstrating to the Egyptians again that He was greater than Kheper, their insect god.

5. When God brought a plague against the cattle and the Egyptians' cattle died, He was demonstrating to the Egyptians that He was greater than their bull god, Apis.

6. When God brought a plague of boils upon the Egyptian people, He was demonstrating to them that He was greater than their god of medicine, Imhotep.

7. When God brought the plague of hail and fire to destroy the Egyptian crops, He was demonstrating to them that He was greater than Nut, their god of the sky.

8. When God brought the plague of locusts to infest Egypt and destroy their crops, He was demonstrating

to them that He was greater than Thermuthis, their god of fertility and harvest.

9. When God brought a plague of darkness upon the Egyptian people, He was demonstrating to them that He was greater than their chief god of the sun, Ra.

10. And when God sent the death angel to kill the firstborn in the land, He was demonstrating to Pharaoh that He was greater than Pharaoh. You see, Pharaoh considered *himself* a god, as did the Egyptian people. His son was considered a god as well. When Pharaoh's firstborn son died, God once again proved that He alone was supreme. Egypt had struck God's firstborn, the children of Israel. Now God would strike Egypt's firstborn.

Ten false gods. Ten plagues sent by the true God. Ten times God showed to the people He was more powerful than everything else they worshipped. Over and over again, God was saying, *"I alone am God. There is none besides me!"*

GOD'S PEOPLE ARE A DISTINCT PEOPLE—SET APART

When each of these plagues came against the land of Egypt, not ONE of them touched the land where the Israelites were living. Not their crops. Not their animals. Not their families.

God spoke in Exodus 8:22 and 23 and said, *"But on that day I will set apart the land of Goshen, where My people are living, so that no swarms of insects will be there, in order that you may know that I, the Lord, am in the midst of the land. And I will put a division between My people and your people."* This is another revelation that God intends for His people to be separate, holy unto Him. Repeatedly throughout Exodus God makes the point of the distinction between His people and the *world*.

TURN YOUR BACK ON ALL OTHER GODS!

When Israel came out of Egypt, and God gave Moses the instruction for building the Tabernacle, He told Moses that the main entrance to the outer court was to face the East. Why?

Remember, the "greatest" god the Egyptians worshipped was the sun god Ra. We all know the sun rises in the East and sets in the West. God was saying to His people, *"When you approach me, when you come into My presence, you WILL turn your back on ALL other gods!"*

Like the Egyptians, we, too, may have many "gods" in our lives: money, power, fame, our job, a relationship, drugs, alcohol, television, the Internet...anything that we place over and above our relationship with God could be considered a god in our lives.

God says, *"If you want to approach Me, if you want an intimate relationship with Me in your life, if you want to experience and encounter My presence and power in your life, then turn your back on ALL other gods!"*

THE ENCAMPMENT

In Numbers 1, God instructed Moses "who" (what tribe) was to camp "where" (in relation to the Tabernacle). So even the positioning of the tribes of Israel in relationship to where they camped around the Tabernacle had meaning, purpose and revelation.

The Tabernacle was to be pitched in the center of the camp of Israel. Everything else surrounded and revolved around it, just as God should be at the center of our lives.

Moses and Aaron were to camp closest to the East entrance to the Tabernacle, followed by the tribes of Judah, Issachar, and Zebulun. These tribes guarded the entrance to the Tabernacle. On the surface you may say, "No big deal. They had to camp somewhere." Is there something more God is saying to us?

The tribe of Judah pitched their camp closest to Moses and Aaron. Many of us are familiar with the meaning of the word Judah: "May He (God) be praised."

The name Issachar translated means "he will bring reward." The Bible says of Issachar that they were men who understood the times and knew what to do (1 Chronicles 12:32).

Zebulun means "dwelling, habitation."

May we today be priests to our God who understand the times we live in and know what to do. May we bring our reward with us to God. May we praise Him. May we enter His dwelling and habitation!

THE TABERNACLE'S FRAMEWORK AND PERIMETER

Numbers are important and significant to God, and throughout Scripture they have significant meaning. God is a God of design, plan, and purpose—a truth that's clearly evidenced in the symbolism contained in the design and construction of the Tabernacle:

The Tabernacle consisted of three sections: the outer court, the inner court and the Holy of Holies. I'll share in much more detail about the mysteries hidden in these areas in the chapters to come.

- The framework for the Tabernacle was made up of 48 boards overlaid with gold, and these 48 boards stood in 96 sockets of silver. (There is so much we could say about the meaning behind God's explicit instructions for the construction of the Tabernacle. The number of boards, the sockets, the meaning behind the gold and silver, but for the sake of our journey I'm going to leave much of that for another time.)
- The perimeter of the Tabernacle was 50 cubits wide by 100 cubits long or approximately 75 feet by 150 feet. Forming the perimeter were fine linen cloths, five cubits high, approximately 7 1/2 feet. The perimeter was a demarcation from the people to the place of service, worship, and the presence of God Himself.
- The perimeter was supported by 60 columns. Silver on the top, brass on the bottom. Each of the columns or posts was supported by two ropes, anchored into the ground to support the outer structure. There are 60 men in the blood line from Adam to Christ (Matthew 1:1-16 and Luke 3:23-38).

- There were 120 ropes that held up the 60 posts. Noah spent 120 years building the ark (Genesis 6:3). Moses was 120 years old when he brought the children of Israel to the Promised Land (Deuteronomy 34:7). In 2 Chronicles 5:11-14 there is reference to 120 priests blowing 120 silver trumpets. There were 120 people in the upper room on the day of Pentecost (Acts 1:5-12).

(Note: It's interesting that the ropes were referred to as hands and had names...the Word and the Spirit. It's the hands of the Word and the Spirit that hold up our lives. Without both, we are unstable and topple.)

The number of columns, posts, ropes, sockets, materials used, gold, silver, brass, and the dimensions of the entrances all hold tremendous mysteries and revelation. Time doesn't permit a full exploration of these in this book but I would like to share with you in the next chapter some significant revelation of the gates.

DIGGING DEEPER

1. After reading about the 10 gods the Egyptians worshipped (and there were probably many more than 10!), consider what false "gods" you may be worshipping in your life. These could be material things, relationships, emotional ties, wrong thought patterns, addictions...anything you may be (knowingly or unknowingly) exalting over the one, true God.

2. Now, make a written list of your "gods," asking the Holy Spirit to reveal what is truly in your heart. Be courageous!

3. God has commanded us, *"You shall have no other gods before Me."* He is clear that His judgments and blessings are linked to our disobedience or our obedience to this command (Exodus 20:3-6). Are you ready to repent for anything or anyone you have exalted in your mind and heart over God? If not, why not? Be honest before the Lord and with yourself.

4. Spend time now talking to the Lord and confessing any struggle you may have with false gods. After repenting, cry out for His mercy and grace in helping you to obey His command to have no other gods. Then praise and exalt Him as the one, true God!

CHAPTER 9

Guarding Your Gates

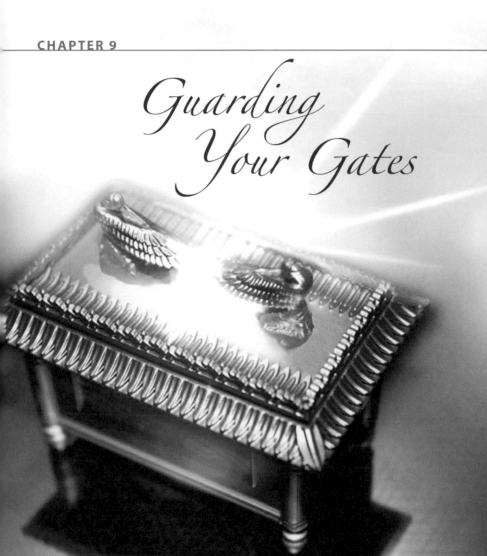

"I have made a covenant

with my eyes."

JOB 31:1

*I*N CHAPTER 6, I SHARED WITH you how God has pictures and patterns buried in Scripture for us to discover. While it may be easier to just sit and read all the great stories in the Bible, we only discover the vast richness buried in His Word when we mine for the hidden "gold."

In coming chapters, we'll examine together the meaning behind the deep *spiritual* truths found in the *natural* reality of Moses' wilderness Tabernacle. Together, we'll look at the structure of the outer court, inner court, and Holy of Holies and the contents they held, and explore how these reveal an amazing pathway into the Lord's presence and His design for our lives.

I want you to keep all this in mind as we pause for a moment to look at Solomon's Temple and the gates that were in the walls surrounding this holy house of sacrifice and worship. Now, you may be wondering, "Gates? How could *gates* possibly have anything to do with an intimate relationship with the Lord?"

The psalmist declares, *"Enter His gates with thanksgiving and His courts with praise. Give thanks to Him, bless His name"* (Psalm 100:4). The pathway into the intimacy of God's presence begins with entering through the gates with His name on our lips and His praise in our heart.

ONE GATE VS. FIVE

As I noted earlier, the wilderness Tabernacle was the forerunner for Solomon's Temple. While the layout of the Tabernacle and Temple are almost identical, there are a few differences. One of these differences is the entrances.

Moses' Tabernacle had only *one* entrance by which the outer court could be accessed. The picture painted for us in this is clear: There is only *one* way for us to enter into an intimate relationship with our Heavenly Father.

Jesus said, *"I am the way, and the truth, and the life; no one comes to the Father but through Me"* (John 14:6). If we want access to God, we must enter through the one–and only–"gate" He has provided: Jesus Christ.

However, there were *five* gates in the wall surrounding Solomon's Temple mount. Biblical archaeologists have named them Barclay's Gate, the Double Gate, the Triple Gate, Warren's Gate, and the Eastern Gate. These gates guarded the entrance to the Temple Mount.

Why five? Why not just one entryway, as with the Tabernacle?

A very practical reason for more gates may have been because the number of Israelites had increased exponentially since the time when they had worshipped God in the wilderness. By the time they were assembling from all over the nation to worship at the Temple in Jerusalem, there were more than five times the number of Israelites, and so they probably needed five times as many entrances just to accommodate the crowds coming to offer their sacrifices and worship.

Another reason could be that Solomon's Temple and the area surrounding it was much bigger than the court of Moses' Tabernacle. This, too, would necessitate having more entrances. Although we can only wonder about Solomon's reasoning in the *natural,* let's consider God's *spiritual* reason for why the Temple wall had five gates instead of one.

Based on 1 Chronicles 28:11-12 (NKJV), we know that in addition to Moses' God-given pattern of the Tabernacle recorded in the Torah, King David also received additional revelation from the Holy Spirit for how Solomon was to build the Temple: *"Then David gave his son Solomon the plans for the vestibule, its houses, its treasuries, its upper chambers, its inner chambers, and the place of the mercy seat; and the plans for all that he had* **by the Spirit***...."*

Since God revealed plans for the Temple directly to David, we can safely assume that the wall had five gates leading to the Temple Mount because God *wanted* there to be five gates. The question is, *"Why?"*

WATCHMEN ON THE WALLS

The responsibilities of the hundreds of priests serving at the Temple were varied, and in future chapters, I'll go into more detail about some of their daily duties. For right now, I want to focus on those priests who were in charge of the Temple gates.

The first thing these priests did in the morning was to open the five gates, and the last thing they did at night was to close them. Night and day, there were shifts of priests assigned to stand guard on top of the Temple wall and at the gates. These watchmen had three primary responsibilities:

1. Prohibit anything unclean from entering.

2. Blow the trumpets as a warning if the enemy was approaching.

3. Close the gates to keep out the enemy and protect the people.

The watchmen knew that these five gates were points of vulnerability through which the enemy could enter to desecrate or destroy the Temple. Should the watchmen abdicate their positions or fall asleep while on guard, the consequences were severe and immediate.

According to ancient Jewish teaching, if a Temple priest fell asleep while on watch, he was either beaten or he was shamed by being stripped naked and his clothes burned. Jesus was alluding to this stern discipline when He said, *"Behold, I am coming like a thief. Blessed is the one who stays awake and keeps his clothes, so that he will not walk about naked and men will not see his shame"* (Revelation 16:15).

So what is the lesson God wants us to learn in the pattern of the five gates in Solomon's Temple and the watchmen on the wall? To answer this question, let's look at these two Scripture passages—one that the apostle Paul wrote to Believers in Corinth and one that Jesus' disciple Peter wrote to Christians living in Asia Minor.

Paul urged Believers,

"Flee immorality. Every other sin that a man commits is outside the body, but the immoral man sins against his own body. Or do you not know that your body is a temple of the Holy Spirit who is in you, whom you have from God, and that you are not your own? For you have been bought with a price: therefore glorify God in your body" (1 Corinthians 6:19-20).

And Peter wrote:

"You also, as living stones, are being built up as a spiritual house for a holy priesthood, to offer up spiritual sacrifices acceptable to God through Jesus Christ" (1 Peter 2:5).

Are you seeing the amazing parallels between the Temple gates and us as Believers?

- The Temple was the Israelites' dwelling place for God's Holy Spirit. As Believers, now *we* are the dwelling place for God's Holy Spirit.
- The Tabernacle and the Temple had three main sections, the outer court, the inner court and the Holy of Holies. Our Tabernacle or Temple also has three sections: body, soul and spirit!
- The Temple priests were responsible for guarding and

protecting it. Now *we* are the priests who are responsible for guarding and protecting *our* temple.

- The Temple had five gates—and so do *we!*

The only way to access the Temple was to enter through one of the five gates into the courtyard. Then, if you were a priest, you would pass through to the outer court, the inner court, and, if you were the high priest, enter into the Holy of Holies. In the same way, we are "accessed" through one of the five "gates" of our body and then our soul, and finally into our spirit.

What are our five gates? Our five senses through which we see, hear, touch, smell, and taste! As God's appointed priest over our own body, it's our job to be the watchmen on the wall of our own "temple." Like the Temple priests, it's our responsibility to...

1. Prohibit anything unclean from entering.

2. Heed the warning when the enemy is approaching.

3. Close the gates to protect ourselves from the enemy.

But sadly, most of us have done a poor job of guarding our own gates. We've...

- Looked at things we definitely shouldn't have seen.
- Listened to things we had no business hearing.
- Touched things we clearly shouldn't have touched.
- Tasted things God never intended for us to taste.
- Spoken words that should never have come out of our mouths.

And then we wonder why we're sick, poor, wretched, and blind. It's because we haven't stood watch as priests over our five gates and our temple, and so we've permitted the enemy to set up camp in our lives. But God has called us to be priests and watchmen on the walls of our temple. He has called us to stand guard against the enemy!

'THE PRINCE OF THE POWER OF THE AIR'

Our heart and mind are influenced (consciously and subconsciously) through whatever passes through the gates of our eyes, ears, hands, nose, and mouth. The failure to diligently guard the gates of our temple has had disastrous consequences for us, our families, our country, and ultimately for the nations of the world. This is because whoever, or whatever, controls our thoughts also governs the principles by which we live.

Our eye and ear gates are probably the two gates that have the greatest impact on our life. By seeing words and hearing images—both positive and negative—often enough and long enough, these sights and sounds go through our gates, and are imbedded in our heart and mind.

According to Scripture, we are a reflection of what we think in our hearts: *"For as he thinks within himself, so he is"* (Proverbs 23:7). Those things we continually expose ourselves to will eventually determine what we believe, how we think, the decisions we make, and how we live our lives.

Personally, I don't believe anything has influenced our thoughts and actions more in the last 50 years than television, and more recently, other forms of media that have emerged in the last several decades, such as the Internet and the cable and satellite industries. Together, these are having a truly alarming impact on our values, beliefs, morals, and behavior.

Why and how do the various forms of media have such control over us?

"For our struggle is not against flesh and blood, but against the rulers, against the powers, against the world forces of this darkness..."

As Paul reminded the Believers in Ephesus, *"And you were dead in your trespasses and sins, in which you formerly walked according to the course of this world, according to **the prince of the power of the air,** of the spirit that is now working in the sons of disobedience"* (Ephesians 2:1-2).

He also wrote in Ephesians 6:12, *"For our struggle is not against flesh and blood, but against the rulers, against the powers, against the world forces of this darkness, against the spiritual forces of wickedness in the heavenly places."*

Paul was telling us that the battles we fight in this life are not fought in the *natural* realm—they are *spiritual.*

When we put all this together, we can see that our behavior, values, beliefs, and ultimately, our relationship to God, are the result of what we have allowed to pass through the gates of our natural senses into our spirits. We can either be influenced by God and His Kingdom, or we can be influenced by Satan, *"the prince of the power of the air."*

THE FROG IN THE POT

The word "prince" means "ruler." According to Ephesians 2:2, Satan is ruling the air and the power that's in it. Why? Because he realizes that whoever rules the air rules the earth. So he has set up his headquarters in the air and made himself *"the prince"* over it.

And what's in the air? Sounds waves, light waves, microwaves, radio frequencies, satellite and broadcast transmissions, and wireless transmissions. This is what the media uses to send powerful messages all over the world. The word "media" means "middle," and the sad truth is that media...

- Stands in the middle between the source of the messages and those targeted to receive it.
- Serves as the conduit to carry the message from where it originates to the person who watches, hears, or reads it.
- Is one of the enemy's most effective tools in his arsenal against humanity.

Satan realizes that whoever controls media—the music, television, and movie industries; print communication and publications; the internet; and new emerging technologies—will rule our hearts. This is why advertisers spend literally billions of dollars each year to influence our thoughts and choices.

What we once called morally unacceptable is now broadcast nightly on primetime television. What the Bible calls "sin" is now considered an "alternative lifestyle." Any efforts to take a stand for Scriptural principles are labeled "censorship" and "intolerance."

The enemy is determined to control sight and sound waves, and because of this, media's messages of darkness have torn at the fabric of society. Satan's goal is to fill the airwaves with violence, perversity, and immorality so that he can penetrate our eye and ear gates, thereby gaining access to our mind and heart, and ultimately to steal, kill, and destroy our very life (John 10:10).

The messages seen and heard through media shape our minds and hearts for good or evil, and every family has been affected by the spiritual darkness attempting to invade our homes. Every time we turn on the television, listen to the radio, or use the Internet, we're potentially *inviting* this spiritual battle right into our homes.

This is why it's imperative that we guard the gates of our temple—and as parents and grandparents guard the gates of our children and grandchildren's temples—against the advance of the enemy. But tragically, most of us have become numb to this spiritual darkness. Instead of being watchmen on the wall, too many of us have swung our eye and ear gates wide open and invited the enemy to come on in and make himself at home.

We've become like the frog contentedly swimming in the pot of water that's gradually heating on the stove. The frog is unaware that it's being cooked until it's too late.

In the same way, the enemy's numbing process to evil is gradual and subtle. The first time we're exposed to something ungodly, we're disgusted. The second time, we react negatively, but we're not quite as shocked. The third time, we watch a little bit more. The fourth time, we watch the whole thing. The fifth time, we're actually using the television remote to look for violent or lustful content to entertain and excite us.

Before we know it, media's darkness has moved through our eye and ear gates and into our heart and mind. This is how Satan uses his seductive powers of the air. Like the Temple guards, we must stay awake and not be found sleeping when on watch so that we will not be shamed by the enemy!

MAKING A COVENANT WITH OUR EYES

I don't know any parents who actually would *invite* someone with a filthy mouth, blatant disrespect for authority, or who spoke, acted, and dressed in a sexually suggestive manner into their homes and ask them to babysit their children while they went out for the evening. However, this is exactly what we do when we allow negative forms of media to entertain and occupy our children's time and attention. Alarming studies reveal that...

- By high school graduation, the average child has watched **18,000 hours of TV.**
- The average child in the United States will witness an astonishing **200,000 violent acts** on television by age 18.
- More than **300,000 pornographic websites** now *specifically* target children and teens.
- On average, children are spending **6.5 hours a day** engaged with TV, the Internet, digital games, radio, and MP3 players or iPods.
- By the time children finish elementary school, most will have spent more time watching TV than they will spend with their fathers in their entire lifetime!

The impact of these statistics is devastatingly clear. Families are being torn apart by divorce, drug abuse, teen pregnancy, abortion, crime, violence, hatred, and so much more. What was once an *invading* spirit of darkness has now become an *occupational* spirit of darkness.

The root of the problem is that, unlike Job and David, most of us haven't made a "covenant with our eyes." Job knew that in order to avoid temptation, he needed to guard his eye gate:

"I have made a covenant with my eyes; how then could I gaze at a virgin? And what is the portion of God from above or the heritage of the Almighty from on high? Is it not calamity to the unjust and disaster to those who work iniquity?" (Job 31:1-3)

David also vowed, *"I will set no worthless thing before my eyes; I hate the work of those who fall away; It shall not fasten its grip on me. A perverse heart shall depart from me; I will know no evil"* (Psalm 101:3-4). Through his experience with Bathsheba, he experienced firsthand the disastrous consequences of failing to diligently guard his eye gate (2 Samuel 11).

We must guard our five gates and refuse to admit anything unclean. When the Holy Spirit warns us of the enemy's advance, we must respond immediately by barring his access to our heart and mind. Like Job and David, we must vow not to watch, listen to, smell, touch, or taste anything that is displeasing to God and disobedient to His Word.

How do we determine what is permissible and what should be barred from having access to our mind and heart? It's easy!

"Finally, brethren, whatever is true, whatever is honorable, whatever is right, whatever is pure, whatever is lovely, whatever is of good repute, if there is any excellence and if anything worthy of praise, dwell on these things" (Philippians 4:8).

GUARDING OUR GATES

God has called each of us to be the priest over our own temple. We are *not* victims! As we choose to guard our gates and stand firm against Satan's temptations, he will be impotent to use the media, or anything else, to influence our behavior, values, beliefs, and our relationship with God.

Failure to stand firm against Satan's strategies not only brings disaster to our lives, but it also blocks us from experiencing intimacy with the Lord. God is holy, and He requires holiness of all those who desire to spend time in His presence:

"As obedient children, do not be conformed to the former lusts which were yours in your ignorance, but like the Holy One who called you, be holy yourselves also in all your behavior" (1 Peter 1:14-15).

The only way we are made holy is through the blood of Jesus Christ, and I'll be sharing a lot more about this incredible truth in the next chapter. But for right now, know that once Jesus' blood covers and purifies our sin nature, we are responsible before God for maintaining our purity through our choices and actions:

"Who may ascend into the hill of the LORD? And who may stand in His holy place? He who has clean hands and a pure heart, who has not lifted up his soul to falsehood and has not sworn deceitfully. He shall receive a blessing from the LORD and righteousness from the God of his salvation" (Psalm 24:3-5).

But keep in mind that attempts to maintain our purity simply by zealously watching over our gates eventually will become nothing more than religious striving and futile attempts to obey self-imposed rules. And according to God's Word, striving to obey religious laws ultimately results in failure (Romans 7). However, when we...

- Rely on God and His Word to overcome temptation (Psalm 119:11)
- Know that He will deliver us from *all* temptation (Matthew 6:13)
- Trust that Christ *in* us is our hope of glory (Colossians 1:27)

"...but like the Holy One who called you, be holy yourselves also in all your behavior"

- Believe we can do all things through Him because He gives us the strength (Philippians 4:13)
- Endeavor to walk in the power of the Holy Spirit (Galatians 5:16)
- Resist the devil so that he will flee from us (James 4:7)
- Choose to glorify God with our bodies (1 Corinthians 6:19-20)

...then we are empowered to continue on the pathway leading to God's glorious and intimate presence, walking in the righteousness of Jesus Christ alone.

Let's continue now on our journey into intimacy with the Lord and discover how the wonder-working power of Jesus' blood is vital in our pursuit of intimacy with Him.

DIGGING DEEPER

1. In your home growing up, how effective were your parents or grandparents as watchmen on the wall to protect your five gates from the enemy's access? How did this impact you?

2. How effective have you been as an adult in serving as the priest over your temple? Have you consistently chosen to glorify God with your body? Why or why not?

3. What do you sense the Holy Spirit may be leading you to do in order to more diligently guard your gates?

4. Read Psalm 119:9-16; Galatians 5:16-25; James 4:7-10; and 1 Corinthians 6:18-20.

5. Spend some time talking to the Lord about how to faithfully serve Him as the priest of your temple. Ask His Holy Spirit to reveal the ways in which you have neglected to do this, and then repent. Thank God for leading you on His pathway to intimacy.

CHAPTER 10

There's Power in the Blood!

"Behold, the Lamb of God who takes

away the sin of the world!"

JOHN 1:29

*F*ROM THE VERY BEGINNING of God's
relationship with man, He ordained the power of a blood sacrifice.
Abel was part of the very first family, and God was pleased when he
brought Him a sacrifice from his flock of sheep: *"Abel, on his part also
brought of the firstlings of his flock and of their fat portions. And the
LORD had regard for Abel and for his offering"* (Genesis 4:4).

As God's Covenant Relationship with His people deepened and
expanded through the generations, blood sacrifices continued to
be at the center of their worship. Noah, Abraham, Isaac, and Jacob
all honored God with blood sacrifices, and while all of these were
significant, the most profound blood sacrifice in the Old Testament
was the killing of the Passover lamb.

SAVED BY THE BLOOD OF A LAMB

Although God had used Moses and Aaron to bring nine terrible
plagues on the Egyptians, Pharaoh still refused to let the Israelites
go. So God commanded a tenth plague: the killing of all the firstborn
throughout Egypt. No one would escape this horrifying judgment
except those Jews who carefully obeyed God's instructions:

"Then Moses called for all the elders of Israel and said to them, 'Go and take for yourselves lambs according to your families, and slay the Passover lamb.

"'You shall take a bunch of hyssop and dip it in the blood which is in the basin, and apply some of the blood that is in the basin to the lintel and the two doorposts; and none of you shall go outside the door of his house until morning.

"'For the LORD will pass through to smite the Egyptians; and when He sees the blood on the lintel and on the two doorposts, the LORD will pass over the door and will not allow the destroyer to come in to your houses to smite you'" (Exodus 12:21-23).

"Now this day will be a memorial to you, and you shall celebrate it as a feast to the LORD."

Just as God had warned, at midnight every firstborn son, daughter, and animal throughout the land was struck dead, from Pharaoh's household to the prisoners in the dungeon (v. 29). Only those protected by the blood of the Passover lamb were saved.

God instituted Passover as an everlasting celebration when He spoke these words: *"Now this day will be a memorial to you, and you shall celebrate it as a feast to the LORD; throughout your generations you are to celebrate it as a permanent ordinance"* (v. 14). Ever since that night, faithful Jews and Believers around the world have observed the Feast of Passover to commemorate when God "passed over" their homes and families, sparing them from the plague of death.

Years later when God commanded Moses to construct the Tabernacle and its contents according to the pattern He had provided (Exodus 25:40), God instituted blood sacrifices as part of the Israelites' daily worship. God made it very clear to the Israelites why blood was a requirement: *"For the life of the flesh is in the blood, and I have given it to you on the altar to make **atonement** for your souls; for it is the blood by reason of the life that makes atonement"* (Leviticus 17:11).

The Hebrew word for "atonement" is *chaphar*, which means "to cover, make reconciliation, appease, purge, or cleanse." God's holiness requires a blood sacrifice to "cover" sin. Because the blood contains the essence of life, its value cannot be underestimated.

Let's continue now on our pathway into the intimacy of God's presence and move beyond the gates into the outer court of Moses' wilderness Tabernacle, which as you will discover, was a very bloody place.

THE BRONZE ALTAR

The outer court of the Tabernacle was a large rectangle measuring 100 cubits long by 50 cubits wide by 5 cubits high (its footprint was approximately 11,250 square feet) formed by curtains hanging from rods suspended on pillars. God designed the Tabernacle to be portable, so it could be dismantled and carried as the Israelites traveled through the desert.

When the people entered the outer court, the first thing they saw was the bronze altar. According to God's instructions in Exodus 27:1-8, the altar was…

- Made of acacia, a very hard and endurable wood
- Overlaid with bronze
- 7 1/2 feet long by 7 1/2 feet wide and 4 1/2 feet deep

The bronze altar had…

- A bronze grate inside on which the sacrifice was laid.
- Bronze utensils made specifically for use with the altar.
- Four horns on each of the four top corners.

- A ring on each of the four corners, with two poles inserted through them for carrying the altar through the wilderness.
- A continuously burning fire.

Leviticus 1-7 describes five different kinds of offerings that were sacrificed to God on the bronze altar, four of which were blood sacrifices. Two of these five offerings were mandatory and were offered as atonement for the sins of the people: the sin offering and the trespass offering.

When atonement for sin was required, the male head of the house brought a spotless goat or a lamb to the priests (Leviticus 4:27-35; 5:5-13). Before it was killed, the animal was tied to one of the altar's horns, and the person who had brought the offering laid his hands on the animal's head to symbolize that his sins and the sins of his family were being transferred onto this blood sacrifice.

After the animal was killed, if it was a sin offering, the priest dipped his finger in the blood and applied it to the horns of the altar. If it was a trespass offering, the blood was sprinkled on the side of the altar. The remaining blood from both offerings was poured out on the altar's base. The goat or lamb was then placed on the altar and roasted and the meat eaten by the priests.

The Hebrew word for "priest" is *kohen,* which literally means "officiating." The priests spent their lives serving God and attending to the responsibilities of the Tabernacle and, eventually, the Temple. They were needed to officiate at the sacrifices and offer the blood to God as a covering for the people's sin. If there were no blood sacrifices, there would have been no need for an altar, no need for a Tabernacle, and no need for the priests. *Everything* in the Tabernacle centered on the blood sacrifices offered there throughout the day.

According to Exodus 29:38-42, each day the priests began the ritual sacrifices by killing a lamb as a sin offering to the Lord and burning it on the bronze altar. The sacrifices continued throughout the morning and afternoon until the priest performed the final sacrifice of the day, which was another lamb given as a sin offering.

The busyness of the activity, the noise of all the animals, the stench from the blood, and the smell of the burning meat must have been overwhelming. As difficult as it may be for us to understand in the 21st century, the blood sacrifices performed in the Tabernacle's outer court were a vital step on the pathway leading into the Holy of Holies where God's presence resided.

Now that we've looked at the *natural* picture of the bronze altar and the outer court sacrifices, let's dig deeper to discover the "gold" of their *spiritual* significance.

A CLOSER LOOK AT THE BRONZE ALTAR

One of the priest's daily responsibilities was clearing away the ashes from the burned sacrifices of the previous day. This was necessary because the fire was never to be allowed to burn out, and accumulated ashes would have prevented oxygen from getting to the fire and allowing it to burn steadily. Too many ashes would have extinguished the flame because the fire wouldn't have been able to "breathe."

What is the spiritual picture God wants us to see here?

The previous day's ashes from the bronze altar represent the past. So many of us haven't scraped off the ashes from the altar of our life. We're holding on to bitterness, anger, and resentment from old wounds, and we refuse to let go as we tightly hold on to the grudges we bear from past offenses.

Through the pattern of the bronze altar, God is saying to us, "Scrape away those dead ashes. Allow My Love to heal your pain. Forgive those who have hurt and wounded you. Repent for your unforgiveness. Cover all of it with the sacrificial blood of My Son, so that the breath of My Holy Spirit can blow again over the flame of your heart."

As you choose to forgive, repent, and let go of the past, the love of God, the powerful blood of Jesus Christ, and the gentle wind of the Holy Spirit will bring you to a place of freedom in Him that you've never before experienced. His joy and peace will flood your soul, and you will be set free to move forward on your pathway into God's presence.

THE FOUR SIDES OF THE ALTAR

As described in Exodus 27, the bronze altar had four sides, and I want us to take a closer look at the spiritual picture that I believe these paint for us today.

1. **The first side of the altar represents the forgiveness of our past sins:**

    "For all have sinned and fall short of the glory of God, being justified as a gift by His grace through the redemption which is in Christ Jesus; whom God displayed publicly as propitiation in His blood through faith. This was to demonstrate His righteousness, because in the forbearance of God He passed over the sins previously committed" (Romans 3:23-25).

2. **The second side of the bronze altar represents our old nature, the "old man" who has passed away:**

    "Knowing this, that our old self was crucified with Him,

in order that our body of sin might be done away with, so that we would no longer be slaves to sin" (Romans 6:6).

"Therefore if anyone is in Christ, he is a new creature; the old things have passed away; behold, new things have come" (2 Corinthians 5:17).

3. **The third side of the bronze altar represents the breaking of sin's hold over us:**

"For the death that He died, He died to sin once for all; but the life that He lives, He lives to God. Even so consider yourselves to be dead to sin, but alive to God in Christ Jesus. Therefore do not let sin reign in your mortal body so that you obey its lusts" (Romans 6:10-12).

4. **The fourth side of the bronze altar represents the offering of our lives to God:**

"Therefore I urge you, brethren, by the mercies of God, to present your bodies a living and holy sacrifice, acceptable to God, which is your spiritual service of worship. And do not be conformed to this world, but be transformed by the renewing of your mind, so that you may prove what the will of God is, that which is good and acceptable and perfect" (Romans 12:1-2).

Just as the bronze altar was the first piece of furniture encountered in the Tabernacle, so is the Cross of Jesus Christ the first thing we must encounter on our pathway into intimacy with the Lord. God's requirement for a blood sacrifice to atone for our sins continues to this day.

Now that we've looked at the spiritual picture of what the bronze altar represented, let's turn our attention to the picture of the animal sacrifices and their prophetic implication.

JESUS, OUR PASSOVER LAMB

The bronze altar and the animal sacrifices were a prophetic sign of the sacrificial death of Jesus Christ as the final atonement for our sins. The prophet Isaiah foretold how the Messiah would be slaughtered like a Passover lamb:

"He was oppressed and He was afflicted, yet He did not open His mouth; like a lamb that is led to slaughter, and like a sheep that is silent before its shearers, so He did not open His mouth" (Isaiah 53:7).

The Israelites' animal sacrifices were symbolic of man's need and God's mercy. Likewise, Jesus' sacrificial death on the Cross portrays our desperate need and the extravagant mercy God has extended toward us. Because there was no sin in Jesus, He became our spotless Passover Lamb.

John the Baptist recognized this when he pointed to Jesus and declared, *"Behold, the Lamb of God who takes away the sin of the world!"* (John 1:29) Like the Jews at the first Passover, only those of us whose sins are covered by the blood of the Lamb will be spared eternal death at the hands of the destroyer.

As we read in Leviticus 17, *"the life of all flesh is its blood,"* and the writer of Hebrews powerfully underscored the prophetic implication of the Tabernacle sacrifices:

"For when every commandment had been spoken by Moses to all the people according to the Law, he took the blood of the calves and the goats, with water and scarlet wool and hyssop, and sprinkled both the book itself and all the people, saying, 'This is the blood of the covenant which God commanded you.'

*"And in the same way he sprinkled both the tabernacle and all the vessels of the ministry with the blood. And according to the Law, one may almost say, all things are cleansed with blood, **and without shedding of blood there is no forgiveness**"* (Hebrews 9:19-22).

The power of the blood Jesus shed on the Cross for us is reinforced again and again throughout the New Testament:

Jesus' sacrificial death

on the Cross portrays

our desperate need and

the extravagant mercy God

has extended toward us.

- *"Knowing that you were not redeemed with perishable things like silver or gold from your futile way of life inherited from your forefathers, but with precious blood, as of a lamb unblemished and spotless, **the blood of Christ"** (1 Peter 1:18-19).*
- *"In Him we have redemption through **His blood**, the forgiveness of our trespasses, according to the riches of His grace"* (Ephesians 1:7).
- *"But now in Christ Jesus you who formerly were far off have been brought near by **the blood of Christ"*** (Ephesians 2:13).
- *"For it was the Father's good pleasure for all the fullness to dwell in Him, and through Him to reconcile all things to Himself, having made peace through **the blood of His cross"*** (Colossians 1:19-20a).
- *"But if we walk in the Light as He Himself is in the Light, we have fellowship with one another, and **the blood of Jesus** His Son cleanses us from all sin"* (1 John 1:7).

Just as the priest couldn't bypass the altar to access the Holy of Holies, we can't bypass Jesus to get to God. Sadly, so many people today mistakenly believe that there is more than one way to God, but this is a lie. Jesus said, *"I am the way, and the truth, and the life; no one comes to the Father but through Me"* (John 14:6).

Jesus didn't say that He was one of many ways to God. He didn't say He was *a* way, *a* truth, or *a* life. No, He said, *"I am **the** way, **the** truth and **the** life."* He was very clear that no one can come to the Father except through Him.

It's vital for us to remember that the ultimate purpose of the blood sacrifices performed in the Tabernacle was to make atonement for the Israelites' sins and lead them to *God.* This is still true today. Without a blood sacrifice, we cannot enter into God's presence. If there is no blood, there is no atonement for our sin, and if there is no atonement for our sin, then there can be no intimacy with Him.

Keep in mind, too, that the sacrifices offered by the priest on the bronze altar had to be performed again and again and again. However, the blood sacrifice of Jesus was the *final* atonement for our sins. Once He was crucified on our behalf, God's requirement for blood sacrifices was fulfilled once and for all:

"Every priest stands daily ministering and offering time after time the same sacrifices, which can never take away sins; but He, having offered one sacrifice for sins for all time, sat down at the right hand of God waiting from that time onward until His enemies be made a footstool for His feet. For by one offering He has perfected for all time those who are sanctified" (Hebrews 10:11-14).

Thankfully, we don't need to go forward every Sunday to get saved again at the altar rail. When we invite Jesus Christ to be our Lord and Savior, His blood cleanses us from our sin and we are forever freed to walk in a loving, obedient, faith-filled Covenant Relationship with Him.

WASHED WHITER THAN SNOW

Do you remember how I shared with you that the first word God gave me in the hotel room was "REPENT"? In response to my heart's cry to truly know Him, God was just beginning to reveal the pattern of the Tabernacle to me. He wanted me to understand that just as the Israelites had to repent with a blood sacrifice in order to approach Him, so did I need to come before Him in repentance, trusting in the blood of Jesus Christ to atone for my sins.

And not only do we need to repent for our sin nature, but as I shared with you, we continually needed to repent for the sins we commit each day. Yes, we're saved. Yes, we're washed clean by Jesus' blood. But Jesus taught us that every day, we must repent of our daily trespasses that can keep us separated from God's presence (Matthew 6:9-13). It's one thing to be saved by the power of the blood; it's another thing to be forgiven for our daily trespasses.

God says in His Word, *"Behold, the Lord's hand is not so short that it cannot save; neither is His ear so dull that it cannot hear. But your iniquities have made a separation between you and your God."* (Isaiah 59:1-2).

Oftentimes, we're waiting impatiently for God to do something for us, but there is unrepented sin in our lives blocking the release of His blessings. Too many people falsely believe that we're under a cloud of grace that gives us license to do whatever we want and then just ask God to forgive us. This simply isn't true. There are consequences to our choices, and we can't choose to live in disobedience to God's Word and expect to have intimacy with Him.

Who does God welcome into His presence?

"He who has clean hands and a pure heart, who has not lifted up his soul to falsehood and has not sworn deceitfully. He shall receive a blessing from the LORD and righteousness from the God of his salvation" (Psalm 24:4-5).

As Believers, you and I have been washed clean by the blood of the Lamb. I urge you to claim the power of His blood over your life each day as you repent for your daily trespasses and walk in His victory over the power of sin.

You know, I love to worship the Lord, and while I really appreciate the contemporary worship songs we sing in church, there's something very special to me about the old hymns. The theological truths they contain are powerful. One of my favorites is "There Is Power in the Blood" written by Lewis E. Jones in 1899:

> *Would you be free from the burden of sin?*
> *There's power in the blood, power in the blood;*
> *Would you o'er evil a victory win?*
> *There's wonderful power in the blood.*
> *There is power, power, wonder working power*
> *In the blood of the Lamb;*
> *There is power, power, wonder working power*
> *In the precious blood of the Lamb.*
> *Would you be whiter, much whiter than snow?*
> *There's power in the blood, power in the blood;*
> *Sin stains are lost in its life giving flow.*

There's wonderful
power in the blood.

My friend, there *is* power in the blood of Jesus Christ! Power to save. Power to free. Power to change. Power to restore. Power to redeem. POWER!

GOD'S PATTERN OF REDEMPTION

"Without the shedding of blood there is no forgiveness" (Hebrews 9:22).

Like the garment Jesus had at His crucifixion (John 19:23), the Bible is one seamless whole. The pattern established from the beginning, and revealed in the Tabernacle and Temple, was fulfilled in Jesus, as the power in His Blood gives us victory and freedom from sin's destructive hold.

Let me show you...

Twice a day the high priest would offer a lamb for a sin offering—every morning at 9 a.m. and every afternoon at 3 p.m. These daily offerings were called the *tamid*. On feast days like Passover, three lambs were sacrificed: one at 9 a.m., one at noon, and the last at 3 p.m.

One of the duties of the high priest was to inspect the lamb to make sure there were no spots or blemishes. It had to be a perfect lamb. Once the lamb was sacrificed the high priest would stand next to the bronze altar and wait until the sacrifice was completed. Once completed, he would raise his hands and stretch out his arms, declaring, *"It is finished!"*

"Without the shedding of blood there is no forgiveness."

Are you beginning to see the pattern? But there's more...

According to Mark 15:25 Jesus was crucified at the third hour (at 9 a.m., since 6 a.m. was considered the first hour). Then Mark 15:34 tells us that at the ninth hour (3 p.m.), the exact time the high priest was standing over the sacrifice of the Passover Lamb—the exact time the high priest was declaring, "It is finished"—Jesus, the Lamb of God, our Passover Lamb, with outstretched arms on a cross and having paid the price for the penalty of our sins, took His final breath and cried out, *"It is finished"* (John 19:30).

DIGGING DEEPER

1. Some people find it offensive, distasteful, or even cruel that God requires a blood sacrifice in order to come into His presence. Is this difficult for you to accept? Why or why not?

2. As you consider the spiritual picture God has painted for us in the ashes on the bronze altar, ask Him if there is any bitterness, anger, or resentment from your past or present that may be preventing you from moving into a place of deeper intimacy with Him.

3. What areas of your life are covered with the wonder-working power of Jesus' blood? In what areas do you still need to apply His blood so that you are freed from the power of sin?

4. Spend time with God thanking Him for sacrificing His Son as your Passover Lamb. Ask Him to reveal any areas of your life—past or present—where you need to apply Jesus' wonder-working blood, so that you can walk in victory over sin. Praise Him for all that He has done and is doing in your life.

CHAPTER 11

Washed BY THE *Water* AND THE *Word*

"Therefore leaving the elementary teaching

about the Christ, let us press on to maturity..."

HEBREWS 6:1

*A*FTER THE BRONZE ALTAR, the
bronze laver was the next piece of furniture encountered in the outer
court of the Tabernacle, and it was placed between the altar and the
entrance leading to the inner court. In Exodus 30:18-21, God gave
Moses these instructions for the building of the laver:

*"You shall also make a laver of bronze, with its base of bronze, for
washing; and you shall put it between the tent of meeting and the altar,
and you shall put water in it.*

*"Aaron and his sons shall wash their hands and their feet from
it; when they enter the tent of meeting, they shall wash with water, so
that they will not die; or when they approach the altar to minister, by
offering up in smoke a fire sacrifice to the LORD.*

*"So they shall wash their hands and their feet, so that they will
not die; and it shall be a perpetual statute for them, for Aaron and his
descendants throughout their generations."*

From Exodus 38:8 we learn that the laver was made from the
bronze mirrors of the women who served at the Tabernacle. Since
there was no glass in Biblical times, one of the only reflective surfaces
they had was highly polished brass. The women would polish small

pieces of brass until they became like a shiny mirror, and these were the mirrors Moses used to make the bronze laver.

After the work on the Tabernacle was completed and all the pieces of the furniture ready to be installed, God gave Moses instructions for consecrating everything to Him, including the dedication of Aaron and his sons, who were appointed to serve as priests. God commanded Moses to wash them in water from the bronze laver and anoint them with oil:

"You shall anoint the laver and its stand, and consecrate it. Then you shall bring Aaron and his sons to the doorway of the tent of meeting and wash them with water.

"You shall put the holy garments on Aaron and anoint him and consecrate him, that he may minister as a priest to Me. You shall bring his sons and put tunics on them; and you shall anoint them even as you have anointed their father, that they may minister as priests to Me; and their anointing will qualify them for a perpetual priesthood throughout their generations" (Exodus 40:11-15).

Our English word "laver" comes from the ancient Latin word *lavare*, which meant "to pour water on, to wash." Although this consecration of the high priest was the initial use for the bronze laver, *all* the priests were required by God's law to wash in its water throughout the day before entering the inner court and the Holy of Holies.

Because their hands would be bloody from performing the daily sacrifices and their feet dirty from the bare ground on which the Tabernacle stood, God's holiness demanded that priests wash their hands and feet at the bronze laver. If a priest bypassed the laver without washing, the penalty was death (Exodus 30:20). That's how important the bronze laver was to God!

Another of the priests' job was to wash the sacrifices after the animals had been slaughtered and before they were placed on the altar (Leviticus 1:8, 13). As we learned in the previous chapter, *"the life of the flesh is in the blood,"* and God had forbidden the priests from eating blood (Leviticus 17:11), so the sacrifices had to be washed in the bronze laver as well.

WHAT DOES IT ALL MEAN?

The natural picture of the bronze laver would be nothing more than a few interesting Biblical facts if it weren't for the *spiritual pattern* God wants us to learn from its construction and use.

The bronze laver is a picture of the cleansing that comes to us as we are washed daily by the Word of God. In his letter to the Believers in Ephesus, Paul writes of Jesus Christ sanctifying us by washing us with the *"water of the Word"* so that He can present us before God as His pure, spotless Bride (Ephesians 5:25-27).

It's one thing for us to be redeemed by Christ's death on the Cross. Theologians call that *justification*. When I went to Sunday school as a boy growing up I can remember my teacher breaking down that big word, difficult to understand, into a simple explanation I have never forgotten. Justification. Just – as – if – I'd never sinned.

It's another thing altogether for us to be *sanctified*. To sanctify someone means to dedicate them by setting them apart and making them holy. At the bronze *altar*, we are justified (made righteous) and our sins forgiven by the blood of our sacrificial Lamb. But at the bronze *laver*, we're sanctified and set apart for God's service.

Do you remember that when Jesus was crucified, the Roman soldiers pierced His side with a spear to make sure He was dead? When they did, *blood AND water* poured out of Jesus' body! (John19:31-35) What a picture this is of how we must receive His sacrificial blood AND be sanctified by water in the outer court if we desire to journey into a place of deep intimacy with the Lord. The apostle John wrote:

"Who is the one who overcomes the world, but he who believes that Jesus is the Son of God? This is the One who came by water and blood, Jesus Christ; not with the water only, but with the water and with the blood. It is the Spirit who testifies, because the Spirit is the truth. For there are three that testify: the Spirit and the water and the blood; and the three are in agreement" (1 John 5:5-8).

Atonement for our sins is made possible through the blood on the bronze altar, and sanctification for our souls is made possible through the water of the bronze laver.

'MY BELOVED SON'

The bronze laver is also a picture of water baptism.

The word "baptism" comes from the Greek word *baptizo*, which means "to wash, to cover with water, or to moisten." At the start of Jesus' ministry here on earth, He was baptized by His cousin John in the Jordan River. As He came up out of the water, the Holy Spirit fell on Him, and God spoke from Heaven saying, *"This is My beloved Son, in whom I am well-pleased"* (Matthew 3:17).

Of course Jesus wasn't cleansed or made holy through His baptism; He was the only sinless person ever to walk the earth, and as such, He didn't need to be made clean. God used water baptism to symbolize that His Son was being set apart so that He could fulfill His God-given destiny. Jesus was sanctified through baptism in the sense that from this time forward, He would walk in God's purposes for Him as the Messiah and Savior of the world.

Baptism is a spiritual picture God has painted for us of how we share in Jesus' death and resurrection: *"Therefore we have been buried with Him through baptism into death, so that as Christ was raised from the dead through the glory of the Father, so we too might walk in newness of life"* (Romans 6:4).

Beginning with the first disciples and then continuing throughout the ages, water baptism has been used as a picture of sanctification, cleansing, and dedication to set apart those who would follow in Christ's footsteps.

THE MISSING DIMENSIONS

It's important to note that the bronze laver is one of the *only* pieces of tabernacle furniture for which God didn't supply specific dimensions regarding its construction. When studying Exodus and Leviticus, we see that God told Moses how big, how wide, and how high to make the bronze altar. He provided the size and dimensions for the table of showbread, and the altar of incense. He told them the size and the dimension for the Ark of the Covenant.

But when it came to the specifications for the bronze laver, God was silent. Why?

Although we won't know for sure until we get to Heaven, I've heard it taught—and I agree—that God could have been saying, *"There are no boundaries and no limitations to My desire and My ability to wash you and set you apart. Come to Me, and I will wash you, sanctify you, and make you holy so that you may fulfill My purpose for your life here on earth.*"

In a later chapter, I'm going to share with you more about how God used both Moses and Aaron to paint a spiritual picture for us of Jesus Christ. For right now, I want us to note that when Moses consecrated Aaron for service in the Tabernacle, God didn't say that Aaron should wash himself off, clean himself up, and sanctify himself in order to be holy enough to serve Him. No, God says that *Moses* was to wash Aaron at the bronze laver (Exodus 40:12).

We need to understand that just as Aaron could not sanctify himself but needed Moses to wash him, so are we unable to sanctify ourselves through our own efforts or works. This is a picture of how we need the blood of Jesus Christ and the cleansing water of God's Word to wash and sanctify us.

Next, let's take a look at the pattern God has revealed to us by having the laver constructed from bronze mirrors...

LOOK IN THE MIRROR

The bronze laver was covered with reflective mirrors because God wanted the priests to see themselves as they washed. The process of sanctification only begins when we're willing to look at ourselves in honesty and humility, and ask God to reveal the darkness of our souls.

James spoke of this "mirror" of self-examination:

"For if anyone is a hearer of the word and not a doer, he is like a man who looks at his natural face in a mirror; for once he has looked at himself and gone away, he has immediately forgotten what kind of person he was.

"But one who looks intently at the perfect law, the law of liberty, and abides by it, not having become a forgetful hearer but an effectual doer, this man will be blessed in what he does" (James 1:23-25).

We have a choice when we look into the mirror of the Word. We can see ourselves as God sees us and then walk away, unchanged, choosing to forget the kind of person we saw reflected there. Or we can respond to what we see by asking God to forgive our sins and to provide us with the strength and courage we need to allow Him to wash and sanctify us through His Word.

It's the Word of God that will judge us when we stand before God in Heaven one day. Jesus said, *"If anyone hears My sayings and does not keep them, I do not judge him; for I did not come to judge the world, but to save the world. He who rejects Me and does not receive My sayings, has one who judges him; **the word I spoke is what will judge him at the last day**"* (John 12:47-48).

"For the word of God is living and active and sharper than any two-edged sword and piercing as far as the division of soul and spirit."

We can come to the Word of God voluntarily and allow it to judge us while there's still time to respond to God's sanctifying process, or we can bypass His bronze laver of sanctification and let the Word judge us on the Last Day. Paul tell us in 1 Corinthians 11:31, *"But if we judged ourselves rightly, we would not be judged."* What a thought!

I don't know about you, but I'd rather look into the mirror of God's Word every day to see how much I need His cleansing and help! I want His Holy Scripture to be the sword in His hand that cuts away every ungodly thing in my heart and life:

"For the word of God is living and active and sharper than any two-edged sword, and piercing as far as the division of soul and spirit, of both joints and marrow, and able to judge the thoughts and intentions of the heart" (Hebrews 4:12).

DO YOU WANT TO GO FURTHER?

It's at this point in the journey that we must pause and make a choice: Do we want stay in the outer court, or are we ready to move on to the holy place of the inner court?

Sadly, a lot of us choose to remain in the outer court for our entire lives. Some of us have never moved beyond the bronze altar. Maybe we've asked Jesus to be our Savior, but we've never developed the Godly habit of repenting for our daily trespasses.

Maybe we've been water baptized, but we haven't moved any further in the sanctification process by allowing God to set us apart from the world for His purposes. We haven't chosen to come to the bronze laver with humility and honesty to peer into our reflection, repent for what we see there, and ask God to sanctify us with the washing of the water of the Word.

Too many of us are content simply with having our sins forgiven. We gladly accepted Jesus' blood sacrifice to atone for our sins and save us from an eternity in hell, but since then we've been content just to camp out in the outer court. We've become comfortable waiting for our *future* in Heaven while offering the least possible amount of personal sacrifice in the *present*.

The book of Hebrews speaks of these two different stages in the Christian life.

One stage is represented by those who remain babes in Christ and don't press on to maturity. Paul said these kinds of Christians are in danger of hardening their hearts, of coming short and of falling away.

The other kind of Christians are those who *"hold fast,"* firm until the end, and who press on to perfection. Paul said that kind of Christian will inherit the new covenant blessings secured for us in Christ (Hebrews 3:4-15; 5:12-14)

Paul taught that we can actually be brought into God's presence by the power of Jesus' Blood:

"Therefore, brethren, since we have confidence to enter the holy place by the blood of Jesus, by a new and living way which He inaugurated for us through the veil, that is, His flesh, and since we have a great priest over the house of God, let us draw near (enter into) *with*

a sincere heart in full assurance of faith, having our hearts sprinkled clean from an evil conscience and our bodies washed with pure water" (Hebrews 10:19-23).

Many of the Hebrews were most probably the early Christians in Jerusalem. Acts 21:20 lets us know that there were thousands of them. Paul was writing to encourage them to *"press on to perfection"* and to *"run with patience the race that was set before them"* (Hebrews 6:1; 12:1).

Unfortunately in Paul's day, and maybe even more so today, there were and are many Christians who, after professing a faith in Christ, come to a standstill. They never leave the outer court in their relationship with God. They never go beyond a 30-fold relationship with God.

Why? Maybe because they don't know or haven't been taught by their pastor that there is more for them in God. Maybe it's because they know there's more but aren't willing to pay the price and do what it takes to move beyond the outer court into the inner court and move beyond a 30-fold relationship to a 60-fold relationship with God and, ultimately, to the place of the Holy of Holies and the 100-fold relationship.

Quite possibly most Christians never venture past the outer court because they have no idea of what's waiting for them in the inner court and the Holy of Holies—so they look *"in the mirror"* and go away, immediately forgetting who they are in Christ (James 1:23-24). Oh my friend, if you only knew the joy, the peace, the union and communion with the Father that's waiting for you in the Holy of Holies you wouldn't waste a minute of time. You'd run into His presence!

For whatever reasons, too many Christians seem content with the thought that their sins have been forgiven. They've come, if you will, to the bronze altar. They've accepted the sacrifice of Jesus as substitution and payment for their personal sentence of spiritual death. But they've stopped short of the inner court and Holy of Holies. They've become comfortable with the *hope* for the *future* with the least possible amount of sacrifice in the present and resist being truly "set apart" to fulfill God's purpose for their life on earth.

Paul saw many Christians in his day growing cold and falling away. Some ran well for a time and then got entangled in the affairs of life.

In my life I've seen many Christians whose knowledge of the Word of God has outpaced their personal relationship with Him. They're excited to know more, learn more but do less. I've found that it's possible for my mind, will and emotions to be satisfied with knowledge, understanding and good feelings without my heart, my spirit being attuned to what God is saying to me.

Sometimes I think we need to be careful not to become content with our religion, our sound doctrine, and our Christian life, because it's possible that our hearts will become hardened. It's possible for us to live in the natural realm and find ourselves walking by sight and not by faith. When we walk by sight we will end up walking in unbelief because all we'll do is look at the circumstances around us in the natural.

What we see in the natural is not what God sees in the spirit. Neither is it what God wants us to see in the spirit. What God wants from us is childlike faith that lives in the invisible and in the spirit. Our faith is the ear that hears His voice.

Romans 10:10 says, *"With the heart a person believes."* That statement is true whether you're applying it to something in the world or to God. It's with our heart we believe.

Unbelief takes us more away from God. Faith draws us near to Him.

The truth is that our knowledge of God isn't enough. Our heart has to be open to receive Him and what He has to say to us in that place of intimacy, in the Holy of Holies.

There's a great parallel to us of the children of Israel who were about to enter the Promised Land and ourselves today in regards to belief and faith versus unbelief and disobedience.

THE 100-FOLD EXPERIENCE

When God told the children of Israel to "go up" and "possess" the land they gave in to fear. Ten of the twelve spies had come back with a "negative" report. It's interesting to me that all twelve of the spies saw the same giants in the land but only two of the twelve saw God. Ten spies had their eyes stuck on the natural while two had their eyes focused on faith and God's ability to deliver the land into their hands.

Unbelief and fear are two ingredients that cause us to be disobedient. That's why God said to them because of your unbelief, because of your hardness of heart you cannot enter in (to the Promised Land)

These Israelites had the faith to leave Egypt but they didn't have the faith to enter Canaan. But when they were tested to see if they would *"hold fast the beginning of our assurance firm unto the end"* (Hebrews 3:14), they failed. They gave up.

When Paul wrote to the Hebrews he recognized that there were Christians behaving exactly the same as their forefathers in the wilderness. They had begun well but some were now "standing still" while others had even "turned back".

In the parallel to their forefathers leaving Egypt, they recognized that God had saved them from Egypt...they were content with the idea of salvation through Christ as Messiah and Savior of the world but they had no desire to press on to Canaan, to the Promised Land, to a life of sanctification, holiness and power. They were content to "camp out" in the outer court. They were content to live in a 30 fold relationship with God.

In Deuteronomy 6:23 Moses spoke to the children of Israel and said, *"He brought us out from there in order to bring us in, to give us the land which He had sworn to our fathers."*

God brought them out of Egypt so that He could bring them into the Promised Land. Jesus brings us out of our bondage and slavery to sin, out of our past, out of sin so that He might bring us into a deeper, more intimate, more powerful relationship with Him.

The children of Israel were glad to be brought out from the bondage and slavery of Egypt even though they often grumbled in the wilderness, but when faced with the choice of faith versus fear... with obedience versus disobedience...with continuing to wander in the wilderness versus entering the land and conquering every enemy before them, they made the wrong choices. They choose fear... disobedience...and continual wandering.

If only they had the faith to see into the invisible. If only they had the maturity to know that anything God asked them to do was for their good, for their best interests, to give them hope and a future, to bless them. If only they choose to be obedient they would have saved themselves great heartache.

The consequences of their unbelief and disobedience resulted in 40 years of wandering—40 years of waiting for the promises of God. Aside from Joshua and Caleb, that entire generation was not allowed to "enter in" because of doubt, unbelief, fear, and disobedience. Instead, they perished in the wilderness without ever experiencing the blessings of the Promised Land firsthand.

Paul was saying to these Hebrews, don't be like them. God has so much more for you!

The call to the inner court, the 60-fold relationship and experience with God, and the call to the Holy of Holies—the 100-fold experience— is a call to sanctification, to holiness, to intimacy, to worship, to power, and to transformation. It is a call to "enter in." It's a call to take the next step...to move beyond the outer court. It's a call to move beyond a 30-fold level of satisfaction in relationship with God. It's a call to cease from wandering and complaining and to enter the life of victory over every enemy. It's a call to serve God in the land of promise.

In Paul's day and still today, there are carnal Christians and there are spiritual Christians. The carnal Christians are those who have found a way spiritually to do something they could never do in the natural world...stay babes.

In the natural world, in all of life, every plant, every animal, and every human being born into this world grows. Unless you starve someone, they are going to grow. Nourishment, rest, and shelter all contribute to growth.

When a baby is born, if you care for it, love it, give it shelter, feed

Where is the desire, the

hunger, the yearning for

more of God, for the

deeper truths of God's Word,

for a deeper, more intimate

relationship with Him?

God has so much more for you!

it...barring some terrible accident or sickness, it's going to grow. I didn't say it's going to mature. That's a whole different discussion. But it's going to grow. Choice doesn't enter into the question of growth.

But in the spiritual realm, many Christians have stopped growing. They have come up out of Egypt, but they have remained in the wilderness of a worldly life, a life of spiritual inadequacy and immaturity, a life of living in their spiritual comfort zone of "going no farther" with Christ.

You see this kind of Christian all around you. They are the ones who are content with salvation. They rest in their particular church's doctrines, teachings, and orthodoxy, its services and formalities, its spiritual political correctness. Where is the desire, the hunger, the yearning for more of God, for the deeper truths of God's Word, for a deeper, more intimate relationship with Him? God has so much more for you!

In Exodus 6, we read about God speaking with Moses and what Moses was to tell the Children of Israel. (Exodus 6:5-8) Listen to the five things God promised to do for His children as He was about to bring them out of Egypt. To Bible scholars, Egypt has always represented the world, the world's systems, beliefs, and behavior. Now keep that thought in mind as you read:

*"Furthermore I have heard the groaning of the sons of Israel, because the Egyptians are holding them in bondage, and I have remembered My covenant. Say, therefore, to the sons of Israel, 'I am the LORD, and **I will bring you out from under the burdens of the Egyptians**, and **I will deliver you from their bondage. I will also redeem you with an outstretched arm and with great judgments.** Then **I will take you for My people, and I will be your God;** and you shall know that I am the LORD your God, who brought you out from under the burdens of the Egyptians. I will bring you to the land which I swore to give to Abraham, Isaac, and Jacob, and I will give it to you for a possession; I am the LORD.'"*

1. I will bring you out from under the burdens of the Egyptians.

2. I will deliver you from their bondage.

3. I will also redeem you with an outstretched arm and with great judgments.

4. I will take you for My people, and I will be your God; and you shall know that I am the LORD your God, who brought you out from under the burdens of the Egyptians.

5. I will bring you to the land which I swore to give to Abraham, Isaac, and Jacob, and I will give it to you for a possession; I am the LORD.'"

What an incredible picture of what God wants to do for His children today! God has a place and a plan of promise for you!

GOD'S PLAN IN SCRIPTURE

Although I won't take the time in this book to teach on the Scriptural truth that Israel is *not* the Church and the Church is *not* Israel, However, Paul made it abundantly clear that as the Church, we have been grafted into the vine of Israel (Romans 11) and that we are partakers of God's promises and blessings to Abraham (Romans 4; Galatians 3).

Listen also to the things that would distinguish God's people from the peoples of the world. Hear the plans and purposes for yourself as a child of God. Here are God's intentions for you, for His people:

- **Exodus 8:22**: *"I will set you apart...in order that you may know that I, the Lord, am in the midst of the land."*

- **Exodus 8:23**: *"I will put a division between My people and your people"* (the Egyptians, the world).

- **Exodus 9:4**: *"But the LORD will make a distinction between the livestock of Israel and the livestock of Egypt, so that nothing will die of all that belongs to the sons of Israel."*

- **Exodus 9:16:** *"For this reason I have allowed you to remain (in Egypt) in order to show you My power, and in order to proclaim My name through all the earth."*

- **Exodus 15:26:** *"And He said, 'If you will give earnest heed to the voice of the LORD your God, and do what is right in His sight, and give ear to His commandments, and keep all His statutes, I will put none of the diseases on you which I have put on the Egyptians; for I, the LORD, am your healer.'"*

- **Exodus 19:4-6:** *"You yourselves have seen what I did to the Egyptians, and how I bore you on eagles' wings, and brought you to Myself. Now then, if you will indeed obey My voice and keep My covenant, then you shall be My own possession among all the peoples, for all the earth is Mine; and you shall be to Me a kingdom of priests and a holy nation."*

- **Exodus 29:45-46:** *"I will dwell among the sons of Israel and will be their God. They shall know that I am the LORD their God who brought them out of the land of Egypt, that I might dwell among them; I am the LORD their God."*

- **Exodus 33:14:** *"And He said, 'My presence shall go with you, and I will give you rest.'"* When we walk in obedience before God, He shows us His favor!

- **Leviticus 11:44:** *"I am the LORD your God. Consecrate yourselves therefore, and be holy, for I am holy."* God commands us to be holy.

- **Deuteronomy 5:29-30:** *"Oh that they had such a heart in them, that they would fear Me and keep all My commandments always, that it may be well with them and with their sons forever!"*

- **Deuteronomy 6:16-19:** *"You shall not put the LORD your God to the test, as you tested Him at Massah. You should diligently keep the commandments of the LORD your God, and His testimonies and His statutes which He has commanded you. You shall do what is right and good in the sight of the LORD, that it may be well with you and that* *you may go in and possess the good land which the LORD swore to give your fathers, by driving out all your enemies from before you, as the LORD has spoken."*

- **Deuteronomy 7:6:** *"For you are a holy people to the LORD your God; the LORD your God has chosen you to be a people for His own possession out of all the peoples who are on the face of the earth."*

- **Deuteronomy 8:10-14:** *"When you have eaten and are satisfied, you shall bless the LORD your God for the good land which He has given you. Beware that you do not forget the LORD your God by not keeping His commandments and His ordinances and His statutes which I am commanding you today; otherwise, when you have eaten and are satisfied, and have built good houses and lived in them, and when your herds and your flocks multiply, and your silver and gold multiply, and all that you have multiplies, then your heart will become proud and you will forget the LORD your God who brought you out from the land of Egypt, out of the house of slavery."*

- **Deuteronomy 10:12-13:** *"Now, Israel, what does the LORD your God require from you, but to fear the LORD your God, to walk in all His ways and love Him, and to serve the LORD your God with all your heart and with all your soul, and to keep the LORD'S commandments and His statutes which I am commanding you today for your good?"*

This is what God has to say about you...

- **Deuteronomy 14:1-2:** *"You are the sons of the LORD your God...you are a holy people to the LORD your God, and the LORD has chosen you to be a people for His own possession out of all the peoples who are on the face of the earth."*

- **Deuteronomy 26:17-19:** *"You have today declared the LORD to be your God, and that you would walk in His ways and keep His statutes, His commandments and His* *ordinances, and listen to His voice. <u>The LORD has today declared you to be His people</u>, a treasured possession, as He promised you, and that you should keep all His commandments; and that <u>He will set you high above all nations which He has made, for praise, fame, and honor; and that you shall be a consecrated people to the LORD your God</u>, as He has spoken."*

If we took a journey from one end of the Bible to the other looking for places God spoke to His children about the kind of life He wanted them to live, and the kind of relationship He wanted to have with them, we would see the consequences for obedience as well as the consequences of disobedience.

DELIVERANCE FROM EGYPT—A TYPE OF THE WORLD

When God delivered Israel from Egypt, there were two stages. First, there was the life in the wilderness. It was characterized by wandering, wants, needs, complaining, grumbling, unbelief, fear, and disobedience. The consequence of this behavior was the fact that God did not let them "enter in" to the Promised Land. They did not enter in to His rest.

The other stage was living in the Promised Land. There was rest there instead of wandering. That was a land flowing with milk and honey, a land of abundance in place of lack, want, and need. It was a place of victory over every enemy instead of defeat.

Likewise there are stages to Christian growth and maturity. There are stages to a deeper, more intimate relationship with God...to truly knowing Him.

It's one thing to know Him as Savior, to have come out of Egypt so to speak. It's a completely different thing to know Him as Paul cried out for: To *know* Him and the power of His resurrection (Philippians 3:10). It's a completely different thing to enter in, to press on to a deeper, more intimate relationship with Him in the holiness of His presence...in the Holy of Holies...in the 100-fold relationship with God that He desires for us!

Today, may God give us the boldness, the faith, the hunger to enter in, to press on—to move from an outer court relationship with Him to the inner court and, ultimately, to the Holy of Holies.

"Therefore let us draw near with confidence to the throne of grace, so that we may receive mercy and find grace to help in time of need" (Hebrews 4:16).

IT'S TIME FOR US TO GROW UP

So what's wrong with the outer court?

Well, as a *first step*, absolutely nothing. Spiritual maturity is a process, and God is very gentle and patient with us. But He doesn't intend for us to be content with the outer court experience. Because He loves us so much, He yearns for us to press in to everything He has for us.

Just as He did with David, God wants to lovingly gather us into the shadow of His wings and shelter us there with His all-encompassing presence. But this kind of intimacy is only possible for those who are willing to move from the outer court to the inner court and into the Holy of Holies.

As I mentioned earlier, a baby can't remain an infant. Either it grows or it dies.

Here again, we have an example of God using the *natural* world to teach us a *spiritual* truth. Hebrews 5:12-13 contains a strong exhortation for those of us who are content with remaining in the outer court with no real desire to mature in our faith:

"For though by this time you ought to be teachers, you have need again for someone to teach you the elementary principles of the oracles of God, and you have come to need milk and not solid food. For everyone who partakes only of milk is not accustomed to the word of righteousness, for he is an infant."

The writer seems to have been saying to the Hebrew Believers, "You ought to be growing but you're not. Why in the world are you still drinking 'outer court milk' when you could be partaking of an 'inner court feast' or dining at a 'Holy of Holies banquet'?"

We need to move beyond the bronze altar and the bronze laver. It's time for us to ascend the steps and enter into the inner court—the Holy Place—and from there move into the Holy of Holies, filled with joy and anticipation and longing for what we will discover there in God's presence.

PRESS ON!

When a builder pours the concrete foundation for a building, he knows this is only the beginning of the building and not the building itself. In the same way, encountering the bronze altar and the bronze laver in the outer court is foundational for having a deeply intimate relationship with the Lord. But our outer court experience is not intimacy...it only represents an essential step on the pathway into God's presence.

Hebrews 6:1-2 urges us, *"Therefore leaving the elementary teaching about the Christ, let us press on to maturity, not laying again a foundation of repentance from dead works and of faith toward God, of instruction about washings and laying on of hands, and the resurrection of the dead and eternal judgment."*

While *"repentance"* and *"washings"* are foundational to our relationship with the Lord, we cannot stop there. The writer of Hebrews instructs us to move on and leave these elementary teachings behind us as we press on to spiritual maturity. We must press on if we truly desire an intimate relationship with the Lord.

The same writer also said, *"Therefore, since we have so great a cloud of witnesses surrounding us, let us also lay aside every encumbrance and the sin which so easily entangles us, and let us run with endurance the race that is set before us"* (Hebrews 12:1). When running a race, the runners must keep running if they want to cross the finish line and claim their prize.

In the same way, we can't stop running our race until we cross the finish line and run into His arms. And my friend, you need to know that the race doesn't end in the outer court.

I invite you to press on in this journey with me as we ascend to the inner court and then move beyond the veil into the Holy of Holies.

This is where God's presence dwells and the prize of an intimate relationship with Him is the rich reward that awaits. Press on!

DIGGING DEEPER

1. In Ephesians 5, Paul talks about us being washed by the water and the Word. Are you spending regular time with God, allowing Him to wash you with truth from His Word? If so, how are you being changed as you look into His Word? If not, what is preventing you from experiencing this cleansing process?

2. Have you ever experienced water baptism? If so, what kind of impact did this have on your walk with the Lord? If you haven't been water baptized, are you ready to do that at this time in your life? Why or why not?

3. How would you describe your level of spiritual maturity? Are you an infant who is content with "milk"? Are you an adolescent who is happy with "hamburger"? Or are you a spiritually mature adult who is regularly feasting on "prime rib" in the Lord's presence? Why are you at this level of spiritual maturity?

4. Spend time with the Lord talking about your desire—or lack of desire—to press into a place of deeper intimacy with Him. If He reveals anything to you that is holding you back, confess it to Him, and ask Him for His strength and courage to run this race with endurance until you run into His waiting arms.

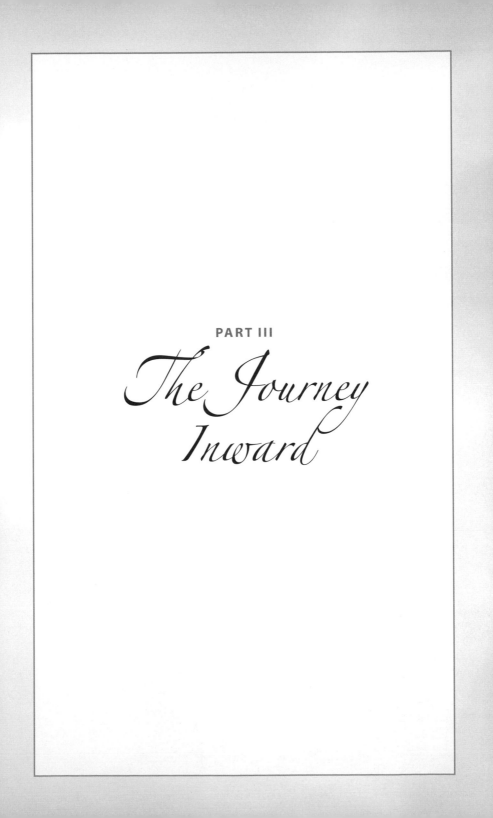

PART III

The Journey
Inward

CHAPTER 12

Climbing the Stairs

"I will bless the LORD at all times;

His praise shall continually be in my mouth."

PSALM 34:1

*W*HEN THE LORD SPOKE TO me that morning in the hotel coffee shop about pursuing an intimate relationship with Him, you'll recall the second word He gave me was "PRAISE." I knew that He was asking me to spend more time praising Him. In the months and years since then, God has continued to unfold for me what He meant through the pattern of the stairs in Solomon's Temple leading from the outer court up to the inner court.

As I've dug for hidden treasure in Scripture, I've come to understand that not only did the priests declare God's praises on these 144 stairs, but God has also used them to paint a *spiritual picture* of how He calls us to praise Him faithfully as we prepare to enter into a more intimate relationship with Him.

Let's leave the outer court behind us now as we press onward and upward to access the inner court through our praises.

THE PSALMS OF ASCENT

I was reading my Bible one day and pouring over the Book of Psalms when my attention was caught by the little descriptive captions at the beginning of each psalm. Some of them read "A Psalm of David" or

"For the choir director." But when I got to Psalm 120, I started seeing captions I didn't understand.

All 15 captions for Psalm 120 through Psalm 134 said the same thing: "A Song of Ascents." I wondered, "'A Psalm of David' I understand, but what in the world is a 'Psalm of Ascent'?"

So I decided to do some gold digging.

The Hebrew word for "psalm" is *mizmor*, which means "a poem sung with instruments." Its root is another Hebrew word, *zamar*, which means "to touch the strings or parts of a musical instrument; to play upon; to make music accompanied by the voice; to praise." So a psalm is a song that is sung accompanied by musical instruments.

I learned that after the priest had performed a sacrifice on the bronze altar and washed in the bronze laver in the outer court, he came to a set of stairs leading up to the Temple, which housed the inner court and Holy of Holies. The priest would stand before the steps and sing Psalm 120.

Then he would take the first step up and sing Psalm 121. He would take another step and sing Psalm 122, and then another step and another step, praising his way up the stairs and into the inner court.

DAVID'S EXAMPLE

While the wilderness Tabernacle of Moses was not a place of singing, music, or dancing, Solomon's Temple was quite different. I believe this is because Solomon grew up exposed to the expressive, emotional, joyful sounds of music that his father David had instituted as a regular part of worship.

When David brought the Ark of the Covenant up to Jerusalem, the joyous processional was explosive with music:

"And the children of the Levites bore the ark of God on their shoulders, by its poles, as Moses had commanded according to the word of the LORD.

"Then David spoke to the leaders of the Levites to appoint their

brethren to be the singers accompanied by instruments of music, stringed instruments, harps, and cymbals, by raising the voice with resounding joy" (1 Chronicles 15:15-16 KJV).

David is credited with writing 73 of the psalms, and, in fact, according to 1 Chronicles 23:5, it was David himself who invented many of the instruments that were used: *"...and 4,000 were praising the LORD with the instruments which David made for giving praise."*

Even after the Ark of the Covenant was in place, the musical praise of God's goodness, mercy, faithfulness, and power continued because David had appointed priests to maintain ongoing worship as part of their daily responsibilities (1 Chronicles 16:4-6; 37).

It was in this rich seed bed of musical instruments and song that Solomon grew and eventually was anointed as king. For him, music and singing were a normal part of worship. This is why when Solomon dedicated the Temple, he had the priests play cymbals, stringed instruments, harps, and cymbals, and lift their voices in unity to praise the Lord: *"For He is good; for His mercy endures forever."* As they did, the glory of the Lord fell, and His presence was so strong, that the priests were unable to continue ministering (2 Chronicles 5:12-14)!

It's no surprise, then, that Solomon instituted the singing of psalms as a regular part of Temple worship, including the Psalms of Ascent, which were sung on the steps leading up to the inner court.

STEP BY STEP

As the priest stood before the bottom step, he would begin to sing: *"In my trouble, I cried to the Lord, and He answered me. Deliver my soul, oh Lord, from lying lips, from a deceitful tongue..."* (Psalm 120:1-2). And then he would continue on, step by step for the next 14 steps:

Step 1: *"I will lift up my eyes to the mountains, from where shall my help come? My help comes from the Lord, who made Heaven and Earth..."* (Psalm 121:1-2).

Step 2: *"I was glad when they said to me, 'Let us go to the house of the Lord...'"* (Psalm 122:1).

Step 3: *"To You I lift up my eyes, oh You who are enthroned in the heavens..."* (Psalm 123:1).

Step 4: *"Had it not been the Lord who was on our side when men rose up against us, then they would have swallowed us alive...the waters would have engulfed us..."* (Psalm 124:2, 4).

Step 5: *"Those who trust in the Lord are as Mount Zion, which cannot be moved, but abides forever..."* (Psalm 125:1).

Step 6: *"When the Lord brought back the captive ones of Zion, we were like those who dream. Then our mouth was filled with laughter and our tongue with joyful shouting..."* (Psalm 126:1-2).

Step 7: *"Unless the Lord builds the house, they labor in vain who build it. Unless the Lord guards the city, the watchman keeps awake in vain..."* (Psalm 127:1).

Step 8: *"How blessed is everyone who fears the Lord, who walks in His ways..."* (Psalms 128:1).

Step 9: *"Many times they have persecuted me from my youth..."* (Psalm 129:1).

Step 10: *"Out of the depths I have cried to You, O Lord. Lord, hear my voice..."* (Psalm 130:1-2).

Step 11: *"O Lord, my heart is not proud, nor my eyes haughty, nor do I involve myself in great matters, or in things too difficult for me..."* (Psalm 131:1).

Step 12: *"Remember, O Lord, on David's behalf, all his affliction; how he swore to the Lord and vowed*

to the Mighty One of Jacob...*
(Psalm 132:1-2).

Step 13: *"Behold, how good and how pleasant it is for brothers to dwell together in unity..."* (Psalm 133:1).

Step 14: *"Behold, bless the Lord, all servants of the Lord, who serve by night in the house of the Lord!"* (Psalm 134:1).

"How blessed is everyone who fears the Lord, who walks in His ways..."

For the sake of space, I've only included the first one or two verses from each of the Psalms of Ascent, but I encourage you to read through all of them in your Bible. Just as they were an integral part of Temple worship that led the priests up the stairs and into God's presence, so will the Lord use these psalms to draw you closer to Him.

Since God uses the *natural* to reveal the *spiritual*, let's explore the meaning of the staircase and how these 15 psalms incorporated into the priests' daily responsibilities represent a treasure chest filled with gold for us to discover.

THE PRAISE PATTERN OF THE STAIRS

The picture of a priest singing praises to God as he climbs the Temple staircase to the inner court offers us a beautiful spiritual pattern of how our praise enables us to ascend from our self-absorption and earthly cares into God's presence.

In Chapter 2, I shared with you how singing, shouting, playing musical instruments, clapping, and dancing are all ways to praise the Lord.

Sometimes referred to as a "Davidic" style of praise because of the joyful expressions he instituted at his Jerusalem tabernacle, these can be powerful sacrifices of praise (Hebrews 13:15).

Sadly, too many of us have been taught that the "correct" way to praise God is to be piously quiet. Did you know that there were many hundreds of years when music in the Church was silenced altogether? In fact, after Solomon died, music, singing, and dancing also died out as expressions of Temple worship. Although there were a few Godly kings after him who reinstituted dynamic expressions of praise, by the time Jesus was born, musical celebration in the Temple had been silenced. Only the Psalms of Ascent continued as a regular use of music and song in worship.

While there *is* a time for us to be silent before the Lord (I'll share more about this later), joyful celebration should characterize our times of praise when we're fellowshipping with other Believers and also when we're alone in our quiet times with Him. As shared in Chapter 2, we must be free to express our praise...spirit, soul, *and* body! Thankfully, the enemy's muzzle and chains on the Body of Christ continue to be thrown off as Believers around the world are learning to sing, shout, clap, and dance before the Lord with all their might!

Remember, God doesn't *need* us to praise Him. *WE* need to praise Him, because in praising Him, we are changed. Just as the priests climbed the steps one at a time, singing God's praises, declaring Israel's desperate need for Him, and testifying of His awesome deeds and mighty acts, so must we take steps of praise every day as we acknowledge that our hope is in Him *alone:*

"I wait for the LORD, my soul does wait, and in His word do I hope. My soul waits for the Lord more than the watchmen for the morning... hope in the LORD; for with the LORD there is lovingkindness, and with Him is abundant redemption" (Psalms 130:5-7).

Only as we climb the staircase singing with our voices, minds, and spirits (1 Corinthians 14:15) will we be able to access the inner court and the Holy of Holies to be in His presence. We must be priests who ascend

God doesn't need

us to praise Him.

WE *need to praise Him*

because in praising Him,

we are changed.

steps of praise, proclaiming the greatness and goodness of God:

"But you are a chosen race, A royal priesthood, a holy nation, a people for God's own possession, so that you may proclaim the excellencies of Him who has called you out of darkness into His marvelous light" (1 Peter 2:9).

BLESS THE LORD

Although Paul wrote his letter to the Believers in the church at Colossae more than 2,000 years ago, his words are alive with meaning for us today: *"Let the word of Christ richly dwell within you, with all wisdom teaching and admonishing one another with psalms and hymns and spiritual songs, singing with thankfulness in your hearts to God"* (Colossians 3:16).

My friend, it's time for us to sing!

When the priest reached the fourteenth and final step, before entering the inner court of the Temple, he would lift up his hands and sing the final Psalm of Ascent from Psalm 134:

> *"Behold, bless the LORD, all servants of the LORD,*
> *Who serve by night in the house of the LORD!*
> *Lift up your hands to the sanctuary*
> *And bless the LORD.*
> *May the LORD bless you from Zion,*
> *He who made heaven and earth."*

As we continue on our pathway into God's presence and prepare to enter the inner court, may we, too, lift up our hands and bless the Lord, and may He bless us with an increasingly intimate relationship with Him in return.

DIGGING DEEPER

1. Is it easier for you to express your praise openly and joyfully to the Lord with your spirit, soul, *and* body, or is it easier to be silent before Him? Why?

2. Is praise a regular part of your personal and corporate worship time? Why or why not?

3. Read through the Psalms of Ascent. Which of these psalms best reflects your heart and the circumstances of your life right now?

4. Spend time with the Lord, praising Him for His wonderful acts. Remember, the Psalms were originally composed as songs. If you would like, pick one of the Psalms of Ascent and make up a little melody in your heart. Sing the psalm to the Lord as an expression of your love for Him. If you'd prefer not to sing it, then read the psalm aloud to Him and bless His holy name.

CHAPTER 13

Fresh Oil

"Your Word is a lamp to my feet

and a light to my path."

PSALM 119:105

*D*O YOU REMEMBER THE third word God gave me that life-changing morning so long ago? After He said that I was to **REPENT** and **PRAISE,** He told me, *"David, I want you to* **WORSHIP** *Me when you come into My presence."*

I shared with you in Chapter 2 how our praise is a joy-filled expression of what God *does,* while worship expresses our love and adoration for Who God *is.* Then in the last chapter, we explored God's treasure hidden in the Psalms of Ascent and how our praise is a staircase that will lead us upward on our pathway into God's presence.

Now that we've climbed the steps of praise, I want to take the next three chapters and focus on our worship of God by mining the "gold" of the inner court. Specifically, we're going to examine the three amazing pieces of furniture contained in this holy place and discover how invaluable these are to our pursuit of intimacy with the Lord.

Because stairs weren't a part of the wilderness Tabernacle, we looked at the Temple steps that led from the outer court to the inner court. But now we're going to return to the picture God has painted for us in the Tabernacle.

THE GOLD LAMPSTAND

After offering a blood sacrifice on the bronze altar and washing in the bronze laver in the outer court, the priest would pass into the inner court, which was formed by woven linen curtains and measured 300 square feet. It contained only three pieces of furniture: the gold lampstand, the table of showbread, and the altar of incense.

Moses had each of these constructed according to the pattern God had given Him on the mountain, and each piece has incredible meaning for those of us seeking the pathway into His presence. First, let's take a closer look at the gold lampstand.

In the outer court, the sun shone brightly by day and the moon by night. But when the priest stepped into the inner court, his eyes would have had to adjust to the near darkness that was broken only by the light shining from the gold lampstand on his left . A description of this piece of furniture is provided in Exodus 25:31-40:

"Then you shall make a lampstand of pure gold. The lampstand and its base and its shaft are to be made of hammered work; its cups, its bulbs and its flowers shall be of one piece with it. Six branches shall go out from its sides; three branches of the lampstand from its one side and three branches of the lampstand from its other side.

"Three cups shall be shaped like almond blossoms in the one branch, a bulb and a flower, and three cups shaped like almond blossoms in the other branch, a bulb and a flower—so for six branches going out from the lampstand; and in the lampstand four cups shaped like almond blossoms, its bulbs and its flowers.

"A bulb shall be under the first pair of branches coming out of it, and a bulb under the second pair of branches coming out of it, and a bulb under the third pair of branches coming out of it, for the six branches coming out of the lampstand. Their bulbs and their branches shall be of one piece with it; all of it shall be one piece of hammered work of pure gold.

"Then you shall make its lamps seven in number; and they shall mount its lamps so as to shed light on the space in front of it. Its snuffers

The Design of the Tabernacle

1 cubit = 1½ feet or 46 centimeters

THREE PARTS

Not drawn to scale

and their trays shall be of pure gold. It shall be made from a talent of pure gold, with all these utensils. See that you make them after the pattern for them, which was shown to you on the mountain."

The entire lampstand was hammered from just one piece of pure gold, with a large center branch that has three branches to the left and three branches to the right, for a total of seven branches.

As I talked about earlier, numbers are important to God, and He uses them to reveal spiritual things. The number seven is significant throughout the Bible and indicates perfection. John wrote seven messages to seven churches (Revelation 2–3). Revelation 5:6 speaks of the seven spirits of God, as does Isaiah 11:2. There are seven continents on planet Earth. And there were seven branches on the lampstand.

Like the bronze laver in the outer court, God didn't mandate specific measurements for the lampstand. However, He *was* very specific about what was to be molded onto each of the six branches:

- Three cups for holding the oil and wicks
- Three almond buds
- Three almond flowers

It's important to note that there was a total of nine items molded into *each* of the six side branches. The center branch had four sets of cups, almond buds, and almond flowers, for a total of *12* molded pieces. We'll come back to this in just a minute....

A PRIESTLY JOB

In addition to opening and closing the Temple gates, offering the daily sacrifices, and cleaning the previous day's ashes from the bronze altar, the priests also had daily responsibilities within the inner court, one of which was attending to the gold lampstand. In Leviticus 24:1-4, God tells Moses what the priests' basic duties were to include for this significant piece of furniture:

"Then the LORD spoke to Moses, saying, 'Command the sons of

Israel that they bring to you clear oil from beaten olives for the light, to make a lamp burn continually...

"Aaron shall keep it in order from evening to morning before the LORD continually; it shall be a perpetual statute throughout your generations. He shall keep the lamps in order on the pure gold lampstand before the LORD continually."

Every morning and evening, a priest would enter the inner court bringing with him a flask of pure olive oil, a pair of scissors, and a pan filled with burning coals from the bronze altar and new wicks made from the used garments of the priests. Once inside, he would carefully inspect the lampstand to see if he needed to...

• Refill any of the cups that might have run out of oil
• Trim any hardened wicks that couldn't draw up the oil (Note: The pieces of trimmed wicks would be taken outside the camp later and buried.)
• Put new wicks in the lamps that needed them
• Use coal from the bronze altar in the outer court to relight any burned out wicks

Why was the gold lampstand so important to God, and why is it significant for us today? Let's dig for the buried treasure hidden in the Word.

'THY WORD IS A LAMP'

As I've already mentioned, according to Exodus 25:31-40, there was a total of nine items molded into *each* of the six side branches. The center branch had a total of 12 molded pieces.

If we add together all the cups, almond buds, and flowers in the three branches to the *left* of the center branch, there are 27 molded pieces (9 x 3 =27). If we add 27 to the 12 molded pieces of the center branch, it totals 39 molded pieces (27 + 12 = 39). Do you know how many books are in the Old Testament? *39!*

Next, if we count the number of all the cups, buds, and flowers in the three branches to the *right* of the center branch, again we get the number 27. How many books are in the New Testament? *27!*

So if we add together *ALL* of the cups, buds, and flowers on *ALL* of the lampstand's branches, we get 66 (39 + 27 = 66). How many books are in the entire Bible? *66!* Amazing! There were 66 cups, bulbs, and flowers in the gold lampstand, and there are 66 books in the Bible!

Since we know God uses the *natural* to reveal the *spiritual,* what is He saying to us in the pattern of the gold lampstand? What's the significance?

THE WORD OF GOD IS OUR SOURCE OF ILLUMINATION!

To those who only want to read the New Testament, or for those who prefer to just study the Old Testament, I say, "You *can't* just focus on the 39 books of the Old Testament *or* only the 27 books of the New Testament. It takes the entire 66 books of the Bible to illuminate the full revelation of God's Word!"

While hundreds of religious manuscripts were written in the first centuries of the early Church, only 66 of these were chosen by the Church fathers to be canonized as God's Word. I've heard of scholars who refer to the "lost books" of the Bible, such as the "Book of Judas" or "The Gospel of Thomas." They argue that certain "Gnostic Gospels" that should have been included were deliberately left out of Scripture.

However, when we discover the pattern of God's Word hidden in the gold lampstand, it's clearly evident that those who were responsible for deciding what to include and what to exclude were supernaturally guided in their selection by God's Holy Spirit. The fact is that God *Himself* chose the number of books He had destined to be included in His Holy Word long before the Torah was ever recorded, the Old Testament written, or the Old and New Testaments compiled and canonized!

When we understand that one of God's significant patterns reflected in the gold lampstand is the illuminating power of His Word, this Scripture verse takes on a whole new meaning: *"Your Word is a lamp to my feet and a light to my path"* (Psalm 119:105).

When we need direction, God's Word is a lamp showing us the way. When we need encouragement, God's Word is a light of hope. When we need to repent, God's Word shines in our darkness. When we need wisdom, God's Word illumines our path. When we need to be reminded of His love, God's Word is a flame of reassurance.

THE LIGHT OF THE WORLD

The gold lampstand was the only source of light in the otherwise darkened inner court. In the same way, Jesus Christ is the only true source of Light in a sin-darkened world. To the woman caught in adultery and about to be stoned, Jesus said, *"I am the Light of the world; he who follows Me will not walk in the darkness, but will have the Light of life"* (John 8:12).

To His disciples and to us, Jesus says, *"You are the light of the world. A city set on a hill cannot be hidden; nor does anyone light a lamp and put it under a basket, but on the lampstand, and it gives light to all who are in the house"* (Matthew 5:14-15). Just as the brightly burning gold lampstand enabled the priest to see in the inner court, as Believers, we're called to be a city set on a hill, shining brightly for the Lost and those seeking to see their way to God.

The olive oil was the source of fuel for the lampstand and represents the illumination, presence, power, and glory of the Holy Spirit from

"I am the Light of the world; he who follows Me will not walk in the darkness, but will have the Light of life."

Whom we draw our "fuel" to provide light for others.

The Lost will be drawn to the Light of Jesus in us as we allow Him to burn brightly in our life. In order for this to happen, we must increasingly be conformed to the image of Jesus, which includes the changing of our very thought process. Paul said, *"Let this mind be in you, which also was in Christ Jesus"* (Philippians 2:5 KJV). We're to have the mind of Christ. We're to think His thoughts.

The lampstand was made from beaten gold, which speaks of workmanship and the process of molding and forming the gold. God wants to mold and shape the lampstand of our intellect to conform to the mind of His Son. The illumination of our intellect depends on the degree to which we choose to yield and submit our will to God's will.

But conforming our thought life to the mind of Christ can be very difficult. Allowing the Light of Jesus to shine through us isn't easy. However, God has used the natural picture of the lampstand's wicks to reveal the spiritual truth for how we *can* be a *"city set on a hill,"* and how we *can* be a light to a dark and dying world.

CLOGGED WICKS

Twice every day, the priest entered the inner court to trim any hardened or clogged wicks, because untrimmed, hard, or clogged wicks won't burn. What is the pattern God is revealing to us?

Each one of us is a priest called to offer spiritual sacrifices to God (1 Peter 2:5), and our body is the Holy Spirit's temple (1 Corinthians 6:19). One of our daily responsibilities is to come to the inner court of our lives where our mind, will and emotions dwell and stand before the spiritual lampstand—Jesus Christ and the illuminating power of God's Word—to trim our wicks and make sure our lamps are still burning brightly for Him.

In Chapter 8, we talked about the vital necessity of guarding our "gates" from the unholy things we've allowed to access our personal temple...sins that "clog our wicks" and block the oil of the Holy Spirit's anointing and power. There are times when we want to come into the inner court and draw near to God's presence, but we can't because our wick has become clogged and the fire has gone out.

How do we light the fire again? We ask God to pour the oil of His Holy Spirit over us again. We act as the priests of our temple and trim the wick, cutting away any part of our heart that has become hardened through sin or neglect. We ask for forgiveness for our sins, and we relight our flame from the coals of the bronze altar of repentance.

Just as the Tabernacle priests had to check the cups for oil, trim the hardened wicks, and relight the flame, *I* am responsible for maintaining my lampstand. If I have run out of the Holy Spirit's oil, I must ask God to replenish it.

I can't expect Him to say, "David, you're looking a little dry, son. Let Me fill you up." This is not the pattern He has given us in Scripture. God didn't supernaturally refill the bowls of the gold lampstand with oil, and He's not going to automatically fill me with His Holy Spirit when I've run dry. Yes, He WILL fill me up, but it's *my* responsibility to come to Him in humility and ask.

It wasn't God's job to trim the hardened wicks of the gold lampstand. He didn't reach down from Heaven with giant scissors and say, "Here, let Me just trim this up." It was the priest's job. And it's not God's job to reach down and automatically cut the sin from our lives. It's *our* responsibility to respond when His Holy Spirit convicts us of sin by coming to God and repenting, trusting in the sacrificial blood of Jesus Christ from the bronze altar to cover our sin.

God didn't grab a coal off the altar in the outer court and relight the lampstand's extinguished wicks. The priest was required to do this, and if we want to have the flame of our extinguished wicks reignited, *we* must go to the altar, confess our daily trespasses, and allow the coals from the fire that never dies to light our wick again.

What are some of the things that can cause our wick to become clogged or hardened and eventually burn out?

- The cares of this world
- Overcrowded, busy schedules
- Our own sin
- Sickness
- Marital problems
- Rebellious children
- Financial crises
- The loss of a loved one
- Shame from past mistakes
- Bitterness and unforgiveness
- Disappointment in God, ourselves, or others

Regardless of why we run out of the Holy Spirit's oil, it's time for us to come to God and ask Him for the fresh oil of His Holy Spirit. It's time to cut away the dead wicks in our life that have become clogged and to get rid of the things that are causing our heart to become hardened against the Lord.

It's time to go to the altar of repentance and receive fresh fire. As we do, we will be prepared to truly worship the Lord...to move beyond praising Him for what He's done and is doing and progress into heartfelt expressions of awe and worship for Who He is.

We've traveled far on the pathway of intimacy leading to God's presence...from the gates to the bronze altar...to the stairs leading to the inner court...and into the inner court where the golden lampstand illuminates and the oil of the Holy Spirit burns.

In this place, we receive a deepening sense of His presence and a taste of the intimacy that awaits us in the Holy of Holies. But we haven't arrived yet. There are still two more pieces of furniture for us to examine in the inner court—two more spiritual pictures to consider—buried treasure for which we must dig.

Come with me to examine the table of showbread, and let's worship the Lord...together!

DIGGING DEEPER

1. Go back and review the list of things that can clog our wicks. Which ones apply to you? As the priest of your temple, how will you "trim your wick"?

2. The oil of the gold lampstand represents the oil of the Holy Spirit. In what areas of your life do you need to receive fresh oil from Him?

3. In order to relight an extinguished flame, the priest used a burning coal from the bronze altar of repentance. Is there persistent sin in your life that has caused the fire of your wick to burn out?

4. Spend time with the Lord. Invite Him to show you what is clogging your wick and then repent. Read His Word to illuminate any dark areas in your life. Pray for the Holy Spirit to be poured out like fresh oil and for His holy flame to be reignited in your heart.

CHAPTER 14

Daily Bread

"I am the Bread of life."

JOHN 6:48

*A*NOTHER NAME FOR THE inner court was "the holy place." The Hebrew word for "holy" is *qadosh,* which means "set apart; dedicated to sacred purposes." While the Israelites could access the outer court of the Tabernacle, only those priests who were ceremonially clean could come into the inner court, which God had set apart as a holy and sacred place meant for worshipping Him.

In this place of worship, let's examine what the meaning in the pattern is for us in the second of the three pieces of furniture contained in the inner court: the table of showbread. Another name used in Scripture for "showbread" was "the bread of the presence." Clearly the Lord was in this holy place. What is His pattern saying to us?

THE TABLE OF SHOWBREAD

As the priest entered the inner court, the table of showbread was on his right, immediately across from the gold lampstand, which would have cast its light over the table. Exodus 25:23-30 provides us with a description of this fascinating piece of furniture:

"You shall make a table of acacia wood, two cubits long and one

cubit wide and one and a half cubits high. You shall overlay it with pure gold and make a gold border around it.

"You shall make for it a rim of a handbreadth around it; and you shall make a gold border for the rim around it. You shall make four gold rings for it and put rings on the four corners which are on its four feet. The rings shall be close to the rim as holders for the poles to carry the table.

"You shall make the poles of acacia wood and overlay them with gold, so that with them the table may be carried. You shall make its dishes and its pans and its jars and its bowls with which to pour drink offerings; you shall make them of pure gold.

"You shall set the bread of the presence on the table before Me at all times."

According to these specifications, the table of showbread was fairly small—only about 3 feet long by 11/2 feet deep and only 2 1/4 feet high. However, because it was made of acacia wood and overlaid with gold, it was heavy and probably weighed several hundred pounds.

The priests were responsible for baking the bread that sat on the table (1 Chronicles 9:32; 23:29). They used the finest wheat flour to make 12 large, round loaves of bread, which were replaced every Sabbath. According to God's directions, the bread was placed on the table in two stacks that sat side by side, with six loaves in each stack. Bowls of frankincense also sat on the table (Leviticus 24:5-9).

When they brought in the fresh showbread, the attending priests were to consume the previous week's bread while still in the holy place. Rabbinical tradition says that even though it had sat for a week, when the priests ate the showbread, it was still as warm and fresh as when they had first set it out.

The spiritual pattern of the showbread is so heavy with meaning for us today that we don't have to dig very deep to find the treasure God has hidden for us in these fragrant loaves.

THE BREAD OF OUR WILL

I believe one of the things bread symbolizes in Scripture is the strength of our will:

- *"By the sweat of your face You will eat **bread** till you re-turn to the ground"* (Genesis 3:19). Through striving and strength of will, Adam and Eve would have bread to eat.

- *"So now also, please listen to the voice of your maidser-vant, and let me set a piece of **bread** before you that you may eat and have **strength** when you go on your way"* (1 Samuel 28:22). Eating bread provided both physical strength and endurance of will to go on.

- *"He causeth...wine that maketh glad the heart of man, and oil to make his face to shine, and **bread** which **strengtheneth** man's heart"* (Psalm 104:14-15 KJV). Bread brings strength to the heart, which speaks of our emotions and our will.

I want to offer you eight truths I believe God has revealed through the pattern of the showbread and how it relates to our will.

Truth #1: The showbread was in the Lord's presence 24 hours a day. We must continuously make sure our will is aligned with God's will and choose to set our will before Him 24 hours a day for His inspection.

Truth #2: The showbread was made of the finest wheat flour, which according to rabbinical tradition, was ground by passing it through 11 sieves. Likewise our will is acceptable to God only when it is has been ground as smooth and as fine as that flour.

Truth #3: Each loaf of showbread had to be molded. Our will also must be molded to His will.

Truth #4: After the bread was molded, it was baked in a hot oven. Heat represents testing. We mustn't think it strange when we go through fiery ordeals; this is simply the bread of our will being tested.

Truth #5: The showbread was put on the table in an ordered structure ordained by God. We, too, must allow our lives to be ordered and structured by God. Without His discipline, we can't be a true disciple.

Truth #6: The bread was surrounded by frankincense. In Scripture, frankincense represents worship. Our strength to do His will comes through our worship of Him.

Truth #7: *Because the showbread was precious, there was a protective rim built into the table to prevent crumbs from falling to the ground. The protection of our will is found in Luke 21:36:*

*"**Watch** ye therefore and **pray** always..." (KJV).*
Our will is protected when we watch and pray.

Truth #8: The showbread was replaced fresh weekly. This speaks of our need to regularly rededicate our will to the will of God.

Like Jesus, we must not seek to do our own will, but rather *"the will of Him who sent Me"* (John 5:30).

FRESH MANNA

The showbread is a spiritual picture of the Word of God.

God required the priests to regularly supply fresh bread for the holy place. This is a picture of the manna He supplied for the children of Israel. The manna in the wilderness is what sustained them and provided their strength and nourishment. Without it, they would have died. Every morning the Israelites would go out into the wilderness and gather the manna needed for that day. If they tried to collect enough for the next day, it *"bred worms and became foul"* (Exodus 16:20).

God uses the *natural* to reveal the *spiritual,* so what is the pattern He wants us to see in the manna?

WE ARE DEPENDENT ON HIM FOR OUR DAILY BREAD.

We must go to Him every day to receive spiritual nourishment from His Word...nourishment that will sustain and strengthen us to do all He calls us to do.

We can't just "eat the Word" at church on Sunday and expect this to provide all the spiritual strength we'll need for the coming week. No, like the Israelites in the wilderness, we must gather what we need from the Lord each day. But sadly, many of us go days, weeks, months, and even years without going to His Word for spiritual strength.

If we tried doing that in the natural, what would happen? *We would die.* And believe me, it wouldn't take months or years. If we didn't eat, most of us would probably be dead within 40 or 50 *days.* We *must* eat to live. Not once a week. Not once a month. *Every day.*

There are serious health consequences when we choose to stop eating or neglect our bodies by giving it a steady diet of junk food.

God placed the natural law of self-preservation in the world. You have to eat to live. You don't need to believe the law, but if you break the law, you will pay the price. There are always consequences to disobedience.

In the same way, for us to be spiritually alive and healthy, we must eat daily from the table of the Lord and feast on His life-sustaining Word. Anything less leaves us weak, malnourished, and our spiritual immune system vulnerable to attack. When we're feeling spiritually weak, fearful, tempted, or distracted by ungodly thoughts, we need to consider that we may be spiritually malnourished. If so, all we need to do is start feasting regularly on the Word of God!

Once again, God is using the *natural* to reveal the *spiritual*. Spiritual nourishment comes from "eating" the Word.

DAILY BREAD

When Jesus was tempted by Satan in the wilderness to turn stones into bread, He responded by quoting from Deuteronomy 8:3:

"He humbled you and let you be hungry, and fed you with manna which you did not know, nor did your fathers know, that He might make you understand that man does not live by bread alone, but man lives by everything that proceeds out of the mouth of the LORD."

Even though Jesus was physically weak because of His 40-day fast, He was able to overcome the enemy's temptations because He was spiritually strong from eating the bread of God's Word (Matthew 4:4).

When the disciples asked Jesus to teach them to pray, one of the things He taught them to ask the Father was, *"Give us each day our daily bread"* (Luke 11:3). Was He talking about physical bread? Yes! Was He talking about spiritual bread? Yes!

Scripture says that Jesus spent time with God in the morning (Mark 1:35) and in the evening (Matthew 14:23). David also prayed in the morning (Psalm 59:16) and in the evening (Psalm 141:2).

Personally, I prefer to spend time with the Lord and read my Bible in the morning. Once my day gets started, I'm going in 50 different directions, and there's just no getting it back, so if I want to "eat" the Word, I have to get up early and spend time with the Lord.

However, the time of day we choose to spend with God to receive nourishment and strength from Him and His Word isn't as important as just *doing it.*

BREAD OF HEAVEN

The showbread also reveals the pattern of Jesus as our Bread of Heaven.

Because they remembered when Jesus had miraculously provided the fishes and the loaves, the people wanted another sign that He truly was sent from God. They brought up the manna from Heaven that God had provided for their ancestors in the wilderness, perhaps with the hope that Jesus would perform a similar miracle. However, He responded by telling them,

"Truly, truly, I say to you, it is not Moses who has given you the bread out of heaven, but it is My Father who gives you the true bread out of heaven. For the bread of God is that which comes down out of heaven, and gives life to the world...

"I am the bread of life. Your fathers ate the manna in the wilderness, and they died. This is the bread which comes down out of heaven, so that one may eat of it and not die.

"I am the living bread that came down out of heaven; if anyone eats of this bread, he will live

"For the bread of God is that which comes down out of heaven, and gives life to the world..."

forever; and the bread also which I will give for the life of the world is My flesh" (John 6: 32-33; 48-51).

Jesus was trying to show them the pattern: *"I* am the Manna! *I* am the Showbread!" but they couldn't understand the *spiritual* because they were preoccupied with the *natural.*

As the disciples celebrated their last Passover meal on earth with Him, Jesus provided them with a powerful spiritual picture. He broke the bread, blessed it, and said, *"Take, eat, this is My body"* (Matthew 26:26). In Scripture, leaven represents sin, and just as the Passover bread had no leaven in it, so Jesus had no sin in Him. The disciples must have been stunned when they understood that Jesus was telling them that the unleavened bread they were eating in the *natural* symbolized Him as their *spiritual* Bread.

In the Church's ancient communion liturgy, when it's time to eat the bread, the minister says, "Feed on Him in your heart, by faith, with thanksgiving." Every time we take communion, we acknowledge that the bread we eat symbolizes Jesus' body, which was broken for us on the Cross. In communion, we are obedient to His commandment to remember Him (Luke 22:19), and as we do, we're recommitting ourselves to Him, as our Savior and Lord.

Just as Jesus invited His disciples to, *"Take, eat, this is My body,"* He invites us to do the same. To *"take and eat"* means to...

- Choose to conform the strength of your will to God's will
- Consume the bread of God's Word on a daily basis
- Feed on Jesus Christ, your Manna sent from God

When we receive Jesus as our Bread, we will find our spirit growing increasingly strong, healthy, and nourished, and like Jesus, we will be able to overcome the temptations of the evil one.

In the inner court, we've examined the gold lampstand and the table of showbread and discovered how together, these form a powerful picture and pattern of the Light of the Word and the Light of Christ, the Bread of the Word, and the Bread of Heaven, and their application to our daily spiritual lives. God wants us to see and follow the pattern.

But there is still one more vital piece of furniture for us to study in the inner court before we can continue on the pathway into the intimacy of God's presence and move beyond the veil into the Holy of Holies...

DIGGING DEEPER

1. Would you describe yourself as a strong-willed person? In what ways have you conformed your will to God's will? What areas of your life do you still need to submit to Him?

2. How often are you "eating" the Word of God? Daily? Weekly? Monthly? Only on Sundays? Never? How have your daily "eating habits" impacted your walk with the Lord and the intimacy of your relationship with Him?

3. "Communion" is a word formed by combing two words: "common" + "union." Would you describe your relationship with the Lord as being a "common union"? Why or why not?

4. Spend time with the Lord. Tell Him how your heart yearns to be intimate with Him. Confess any areas of your life that you're afraid or unwilling to submit to His will and cry out for His courage, grace, and strength to help you. Ask God to show you where, how, and when He wants you to feed on His Word every day, and then joyfully begin to feast!

CHAPTER 15

A Sweet-Smelling Sacrifice

"May my prayer be counted as incense before You;

The lifting up of my hands as the evening offering."

PSALM 141:2

*W*HILE THE OUTER COURT was a
place of noise and activity, the inner court was a place of quiet and
stillness. Apart from the few responsibilities the priest needed to
attend to, there wasn't much to do. Busyness in the inner court wasn't
a problem.

Here the priest's spirit could more easily be at rest. Here, he could
kneel quietly in reverential awe before the Most High. Here, he could
almost hear the prophet's words: *"The Lord is in His holy temple. Let
all the earth be silent before Him"* (Habakkuk 2:20).

The inner court was a place for worship—but not for joyous
celebration with singing, clapping, and dancing. Rather the inner
court was a place of silence, which in itself can be a form of worship.
Even Heaven is sometimes a place of silent worship...

*"When the Lamb broke the seventh seal, there was silence in heaven
for about half an hour. And I saw the seven angels who stand before
God, and seven trumpets were given to them.*

*"Another angel came and stood at the altar, holding a golden censer;
and much incense was given to him, so that he might add it to the prayers
of all the saints on the golden altar which was before the throne.*

"And the smoke of the incense, with the prayers of the saints, went up before God out of the angel's hand."

From this passage in Revelation 8:1-4, we discover that there is a golden altar and *"much incense"* in Heaven's Temple. We also know from Exodus 30 that there was a golden altar and incense in the inner court of the earthly Tabernacle. Since Heaven is where God gave Moses the pattern for building the wilderness Tabernacle, it makes perfect sense that there would be a golden altar and incense in the holy place as well.

And it's to this golden altar and the incense of the inner court that we now turn our attention.

THE ALTAR OF INCENSE

When the priest entered the inner court of the Tabernacle, the gold lampstand was to his left, the golden table of showbread was to his right directly across from the lampstand, and the golden altar of incense was straight ahead in front of the veil leading to the Holy of Holies.

God provided Moses with detailed instructions regarding the building of the golden altar, which are found in Exodus 30:1-10. The altar of incense…

- Was made of acacia wood and overlaid with gold
- Formed a perfect square of 1 1/2 feet by 1 1/2 feet and was 3 feet tall (one cubit by one cubit by one and a half cubits)
- Had a crown molding around the top edge
- Had a horn on each of the four corners of the top edge
- Had gold rings and acacia poles overlaid with gold for transporting it

The priest would put coals taken from the bronze altar in the outer court into a pan and bring it into the inner court with him in order to relight any extinguished wicks on the gold lampstand, then he would add more coals to the ones already burning on the altar of incense. Every morning and evening while the sin offerings were being sacrificed in the outer court, the priest added more coals and incense to the altar in the inner court.

As with the fire on the bronze altar, the fire on the golden altar of the inner court was never allowed to burn out. Incense was to arise continually before God day and night. Historians report that those who were downwind from the Israelite camp could smell the fragrance from the incense from miles away, which indicates just how much incense burned on this altar night and day.

Once a year on the Day of Atonement, the high priest atoned for the sins of the people by taking blood from the sin offering sacrificed on the bronze altar in the outer court and putting it on each of the horns on the four corners of the altar of incense. This was the only sign of sacrifice made on this inner court altar: burnt offerings, grain offerings, and drink offerings were reserved for the outer court altar alone. The only thing to be offered on the altar of incense was incense.

God also provided detailed instructions for the ingredients of the incense burned on the golden altar.

INCENSE INGREDIENTS

Exodus 30:34-37 provides a description of the incense:

"Then the LORD said to Moses, 'Take for yourself spices, stacte and onycha and galbanum, spices with pure frankincense; there shall be an equal part of each. With it you shall make incense, a perfume, the work of a perfumer, salted, pure, and holy.

"'You shall beat some of it very fine, and put part of it before the testimony in the tent of meeting where I will meet with you; it shall be most holy to you. The incense which you shall make, you shall not make in the same proportions for yourselves; it shall be holy to you for the LORD.'"

On the Day of Atonement, in addition to anointing the horns of the gold altar with blood from the outer court sacrifice, the high priest would take coals from the altar of incense and handfuls of incense into the Holy of Holies so that a cloud of incense would cover God's mercy seat. Doing so prevented the priest's death (Leviticus 16:12-13).

As with the other pieces of furniture in the inner court, the golden altar and the incense it held are full of buried treasure. Let's dig for the pattern and discover the mysteries God has provided with this powerful picture.

PURSUING THE PATTERN

The altar of incense represents our worship offered up to God. Just as the altar's incense was to rise continuously before Him, so are our prayers to arise unceasingly to the Lord.

"May my prayer be counted as incense before You; the lifting up of my hands as the evening offering" (Psalm 141:2).

"Pray without ceasing" (1 Thessalonians 5:17).

"Evening and morning and at noon, I will pray, and cry aloud, and He shall hear my voice" (Psalm 55:17).

The Israelites trusted that God would hear and respond to the prayers offered on their behalf by the priest in this holy place. In fact, it was at the altar of incense in Solomon's Temple where one of their priests had a dramatic spiritual encounter, which testified that God considered the gold altar to indeed be a significant place of prayer...

Serving as a priest in the inner court was a rare honor that was decided by lot. Because Zacharias wasn't a high priest, this may very well have been his only opportunity to be so close to God's presence and pray before the altar of incense. As Zacharias was performing his priestly duties by adding incense to the altar and interceding for the people, he also could have been praying fervently for God to miraculously intervene in the barrenness that he and his wife Elizabeth had suffered for many years.

The angel Gabriel suddenly appeared to Zacharias beside the altar of incense and prophesied the birth of a son, who would eventually be known in Scripture and throughout the ages as John the Baptist. The first words Gabriel said were, *"Do not be afraid Zacharias, **for your petition has been heard...**"*

We, too, can trust that as we go to the altar of incense within the inner court of our personal temple and minister there as a priest before God, our prayers and intercession arise to Him. He hears and He responds to the prayers of those of us who love Him and cry out for His mercy and intervention in the midst of our need:

"O God, hasten to deliver me; O LORD, hasten to my help! Let those be ashamed and humiliated who seek my life; let those be turned back and dishonored who delight in my hurt. Let those be turned back because of their shame who say, 'Aha, aha!'

"Let all who seek You rejoice and be glad in You; and let those who love Your salvation say continually, 'Let God be magnified.' But I am afflicted and needy; hasten to me, O God! You are my help and my deliverer; O LORD, do not delay" (Psalm 70:1-5).

Like David, cry out to God *"evening, and morning, and at noon,"* and trust that He is your Help and your Deliverer who will come to your aid.

A RECIPE FOR INTERCESSION

There is a fascinating story in Numbers 16 about the incense from

"The LORD will

command His

lovingkindness

in the daytime;

and His song

will be with me

in the night, a

prayer to the

God of my life."

the gold altar and the impact it had as a symbol of intercession. The people had turned against Moses and Aaron. Because of their murmuring and accusation, God had sent a plague to destroy them. He warned Moses and Aaron to get away from the people to protect themselves, but the two men responded by falling on their faces before Him.

Then, instead of running away *from* the people, Moses told Aaron to go quickly and get fire and incense from the altar and run *to* the people. Aaron immediately obeyed, and as he ran into their midst with the incense, the plague stopped. What stopped the plague? The incense. Clearly God considered this to be powerful stuff!

But for many years, I would read the recipe given in Exodus 30 for the incense used on the golden altar, and I must confess that I never really understood its importance:

"Take for yourself spice—stacte and onycha and galbanum, spices with pure frankincense; there shall be an equal amount of each. With it you shall make incense, a perfume, the work of a perfumer, salted, pure, and holy" (vs. 34-35).

However, my understanding changed the day my good friend and Bible scholar Dick Reuben explained to me that each of the five ingredients had special significance. I now realize that through these spices, God had hidden yet another marvelous pattern in His Word from which we can learn and grow in intimacy with Him.

Although later rabbinical teachings list 11—or even 13—different spices, so that we can unearth the treasure God specifically included in His Word, we're going to limit our brief study here to the five ingredients listed in Exodus 30:

STACTE

Stacte is a resin that freely oozes out of a myrrh tree (like sap from a pine tree). Harvesters could come along and simply scrape it off. They didn't have to drill into the tree to reach the sap; it just came out naturally.

What's the pattern?

God desires that our worship and prayers flow from us freely. He doesn't want to *make* us adore Him or talk to Him. He doesn't want a pastor or a teacher to make us honor Him or intercede before Him. God desires our love for Him to be so great and so overwhelming that worship and prayer "oozes" out of us spontaneously. He wants it to be so "natural" to us that it feels unnatural if we *don't* do it.

ONYCHA

Onycha comes from a shellfish found deep in the Red Sea. When properly prepared, onycha enhances the other ingredients in an incense mixture.

What's the pattern?

God wants our worship and prayers to come from the very depths of our heart. The psalmist said, *"Deep calls to deep at the sound of Your waterfalls; all Your breakers and Your waves have rolled over me. The LORD will command His lovingkindness in the daytime; and His song will be with me in the night, a prayer to the God of my life"* (Psalm 42:7-8). As we intercede before God with deep groanings (Romans 8:26), His lovingkindness will wash over us.

GALBANUM

Galbanum is a plant from the family of umbelliferae, originating in Persia and common in the Amanus regions of Syria. When a branch is broken, it spontaneously produces a milky juice which, when dried, takes the form of a pale, waxy yellow-green gum resin.

What's the pattern?

The significance in this pattern to our prayer and worship life is the word, "spontaneously." Too often we allow the painful circumstance in our life to cause us to turn away from God in anger and bitterness. But His heart's desire is for us to bring Him our brokenness and give it to Him. It's from those broken places that the sweet incense of Christ can arise as a sacrifice of praise.

PURE FRANKINCENSE

Frankincense, sometimes called olibanum, is an aromatic resin. It also comes from a split in a branch and is tapped from a slash in a boswellia tree. And unlike galbanum, which begins oozing from the cut right away, frankincense takes many hours to make its way to the surface of the tree and only happens in the early morning hours. Tapping is done two to three times a year, with the final tap producing the purest form and most intense aroma.

What's the pattern?

Although our human nature is to avoid wounding and sorrow, it's this very process that produces the finest of incense. When, like Job, we can say, *"Though he slay me, yet will I trust in him"* (Job 13:15 KJV), our worship is as pure incense to Him. When everything is still and quiet and we're alone with Him, He will minister His comfort and love to us, and we can minister our trust and love to Him in return.

SALT

Salt has been recognized throughout the centuries as a flavor enhancer, purifier, and preservative.

What's the pattern?

God has called us to be the salt of the earth (Matthew 5:13). As we live out our lives in faithfulness before God and others, and as our worship and prayers arise to Him from the altar of incense within us, He will use us to "salt" those around us.

A FINE BEATING

God's instructions to Moses were to take the stacte, onycha, galbanum, frankincense, and salt and *"beat some of it very fine"* (Exodus 30:36). This means that once the resins had dried, they needed to be ground into a fine powder. This involved a crushing process that required the perfumer to exert heavy pressure using a mortar and pestle as grinding tools. The perfumer would grind the four ingredients individually until they had been pulverized to a fine dust. Then they would be mixed together with salt and allowed to age so that their various aromas could blend and intensify.

Most of us have experienced circumstances in life where we feel as though God is the Perfumer who has us in a mortar and is grinding us and grinding us until we feel as though we've been reduced to powder. All we desperately want is for the pressure to let up and for the crushing to stop.

When we're walking through a season like this in our lives, it's easy to question if God truly loves us. His compassion seems distant and His mercy nonexistent. But this is not true. God's love for us never ends. His compassion never fails. His mercy is new every morning. His faithfulness toward us is great (Lamentations 3:22-23).

According to Isaiah 53, God deliberately and purposefully allowed His only Son to endure the "fine beating" of the Perfumer's mortar and pestle. Jesus was *"smitten ...afflicted...pierced...crushed ..."* (Isaiah 53:4-12). Why? Because God enjoyed seeing Jesus suffer? No! Because He took delight in His Son's pain? No! He knew that through the suffering and pain, Jesus would become a sweet-smelling sacrifice that would save the world.

It's so important to note that Jesus wasn't a victim. He *chose* to undergo the crushing process, because He knew the joy that awaited Him. He could have said no. He could have refused. He could have walked away. But instead, He chose to submit Himself to His Father's will, and because He did, we have the promise of everlasting life with Him.

Like Jesus, we are not victims. We can choose to submit to God's will and allow Him to use the circumstances of our life and the hardships we encounter to transform us into a fine fragrance, or we can refuse and choose to become fearful, angry, resentful, and bitter. He wants our worship to come forth freely, not in spite of, but because of the piercings, sorrows, and crushing we undergo. He is preparing us to be the incense that, when placed upon the gold altar of our lives, will arise before Him as a sweet-smelling aroma and be consumed in His presence.

As the priests of our temple, it's up to us to offer our lives as incense to Him and place ourselves as this incense on the golden altar of our heart. God won't force us to become as a sweet-smelling sacrifice to Him. This isn't the pattern He's provided in Scripture. Take a look and you will see that God did very little in the Tabernacle. The priests offered the sacrifices. The priests tended to the golden lamp stand. The priests made the bread. The priests put the incense on the altar.

God doesn't create an atmosphere of worship...we do. So often we wait for God to show up in our quiet times or in our worship services at church, and we're disappointed when it doesn't seem as though He's put in an appearance. But it's up to *us* to create an atmosphere of worship for God.

This is the pilgrimage I've been on ever since that morning in the hotel when I cried out to Him, "Lord, I want to know You. I don't want just to know *about* You...I want to *know* You!"

When we examine the combination of these ingredients and compare them to the pattern God has established for our prayer life, He is saying He wants our worship to come freely. He's not looking for a parade leader in the church who tells us when to stand up, speak up, raise our hands, sit down, sing praise, or pray. Instead He wants our worship to simply flow from the depths of our heart...from our brokenness...and from our piercings and sorrows....on a daily basis.

I believe God wants us to prepare ourselves as the priests prepared the incense. Not for our crushing but so that we can be a sweet smelling aroma and fragrance before the Lord. Then when we put our incense on the altar, it will rise up before Him as a sweet smelling aroma and be consumed by the coals from the fire on the altar of our heart.

Incense was a type of glory that filled the house of God. Incense is something we offer on the altar. God didn't do it. God did very little in the Tabernacle or Temple. Look at the pattern. Look at the picture. The *priests* offered the sacrifices. The *priests* washed the sacrifices and themselves. The *priests* tended to the golden lampstand. The *priests* made and changed the bread on the table of showbread. The *priests* put the incense on the altar. God simply allowed His presence to fill the place so His glory could be revealed.

The atmosphere that we create through our prayers and worship is created by us but it is created *for* God. We create the atmosphere for God.

GOLDEN BOWLS OF INCENSE

Jesus told us to store up for ourselves treasure in Heaven (Matthew 6:20). I believe that all of the Israelites' worship...all of the priests' prayers and intercession...all of the incense from the gold altar ...and all of the worship, prayers, intercession, and incense that we have offered to God have been preserved in Heaven for eternity:

"When He had taken the book, the four living creatures and the twenty-four elders fell down before the Lamb, each one holding a harp and golden bowls full of incense, which are the prayers of the saints....

"Another angel came and stood at the altar, holding a golden censer; and much incense was given to him, so that he might add it to the prayers of all the saints on the golden altar which was before the throne. And the smoke of the incense, with the prayers of the saints, went up before God out of the angel's hand" (Revelation 5:8; 8:3-4).

As we endure crushing, hardship, and pain in this life, may we continue to make sacrifices of praise to Him, remembering that...

"For this reason I also suffer these things, but I am not ashamed; for I know whom I have believed and I am convinced that He is able to guard

what I have entrusted to Him until that day" (2 Timothy 1:12-13).

Amen.

BEYOND THE VEIL

Well my friend, we have journeyed far together on this pathway into God's presence. We have come through the gates, and into the outer court with the bronze altar and the bronze laver. We have climbed the Stairs of Ascent and moved into the inner court with the gold lampstand, the table of showbread, and the altar of incense.

And now the veil and what lies beyond awaits us...

As we prepare to journey even further into intimacy with God, know that we can only enter into the Holy of Holies because of Jesus Christ, our high priest who leads the way.

DIGGING DEEPER

1. Of the five incense ingredients listed in Exodus 30, which one best describes who you are and your life experiences? Why?

2. Describe a time when you felt as though God were the Perfumer and you were being finely ground with His mortar and pestle. During that season, was it hard for you to believe in God's love, compassion, mercy, and faithfulness? Why or why not?

3. Do you ever feel like a victim because of your circumstances? Read Romans 8:37. How can you apply this truth to your life?

4. Spend time with God worshipping Him. Tell Him your thoughts and emotions about being as incense to Him. Confess any fear, anger, resentment or bitterness you may have toward Him. Ask Him to show you how He wants you to create an atmosphere of worship so that you can be blessed by His presence.

PART IV

The Journey's Reward

CHAPTER 16

Our High Priest

"But when Christ appeared as a high priest...

He entered the holy place once for all."

HEBREWS 9:11-12

*S*o far in our journey together on the pathway leading to God's presence, we've explored how our journey begins as we pass through the "gates" leading to our body, soul, and spirit. We've dug for the buried treasure and hidden mysteries in the "outer court," where we receive the atoning blood of Jesus' sacrifice on the "bronze altar" of our heart. At the "bronze laver," we experience the lifelong process of being made holy as we're *"washed by the water and the Word"* (Ephesians 5:26).

Our journey has continued as we've explored God's pictures and patterns with the "stairway of praise," and then moved on into the holy place of the "inner court" of our heart, where the "golden lampstand" shines the light of God's Word, we're nourished by Jesus, our "living Bread," and we become as "incense" to God, offering up our worship and intercession before Him. We've moved beyond the outer court and the 30-fold experience. We've moved beyond the inner court and the 60-fold experience.

Having come this far, the only thing that would keep us from truly experiencing the intimacy of God's presence in the 100-fold experience is the veil separating the inner court from the Holy of Holies. In the wilderness Tabernacle and in Solomon's Temple, the only person permitted to go beyond the veil was the high priest.

How sad it would be...how desperate our longing would be... if we were destined to forever remain in the inner court and were forbidden to enter the Holy of Holies where God's presence dwells. But thankfully, we have a high priest Who has torn the veil away so that we can abide forever in intimacy with Him!

But before we move beyond the veil into this awesome place of deep and abiding intimacy with the One whose greatest desire is be known and loved by us, there is still more treasure buried in Scripture, more mysteries I want us to discover together.

PICTURES, PATTERNS, MYSTERIES, AND TYPES

By now you have a clear understanding of how God uses the *natural* to reveal the *spiritual.* He uses the pictures and patterns buried in His Word to reveal the mysteries of the treasure He's hidden there.

Another name for these pictures and patterns is "types." When searching for the "types" found in Scripture, we can study the history of God's people in the Old Testament in order to learn truths that apply to the revelation of Jesus Christ in the New Testament. These are truths God has deliberately and purposefully included in His Word so that we can uncover the deep meaning He wants us to understand and apply to our lives today.

For example, Moses was a "type" of Christ. Just as Moses was the leader of God's chosen people, so is Jesus Christ our leader and the head of the Church. Just as Moses led the Israelites out of slavery and into a new land according to God's Covenant with their father Abraham, so does Jesus set us free from the bondage of our enemy and bring us into a place full of promise and hope as we live in a Covenant Relationship with our Heavenly Father.

Whereas Moses was the author of the law, Jesus was the author of the Gospel of grace and mercy. Moses was a mediator between the Israelites and God, and Jesus is the mediator between God and all of mankind. Moses was the first great prophet, and Jesus Himself is the testimony of the *"spirit of prophecy"* (Revelation 19:10).

Through this example, we can clearly see how God established Moses as a "type" of Christ. Now let's look at another type in Scripture that has great significance for us as we prepare to enter the Holy of Holies and encounter God's presence.

DAY OF ATONEMENT

When God gave Moses the pattern for building the Tabernacle, He also provided specific instructions for Aaron's service as the first high priest over the Israelites (Exodus 28-29; 30:22-33; 39; Leviticus 7:28-9:24; 16:1-34). God outlined detailed directions for what Aaron was to wear, how he was to be consecrated, how to perform the sacrifices, and when he was permitted to go into the Holy of Holies.

Just as in Old Testament times, the Day of Atonement is still observed today prior to the Feast of Tabernacles during September or October on our Gregorian calendar. This day is considered the holiest day of the year when Jews and Believers around the world set aside 24 hours to fast, pray, and repent for the sins that have been committed against God.

However, when the Tabernacle and the Temple were still places of worship and sacrifice, the solemn observation of the Day of Atonement also included animal sacrifices, purification, and the anointing of God's mercy seat inside the Holy of Holies with blood from the animals that had been slain.

We learned in Chapter 10 that there is power in the blood, because the *life* is in the blood (Leviticus 17:11) and without the shedding of blood, there is no forgiveness for sin (Hebrews 9:22). God's holy standard required that blood be shed in order for the Israelites sins to be forgiven, and as the high priest, Aaron alone bore the burden of performing the sacrifices first to atone for his own sins and then for the sins of the people (Leviticus 16:6-17).

No one was to be in the Tabernacle when Aaron entered the Holy of Holies, and even Aaron himself couldn't come into God's holy presence any time he wanted, but only on the Day of Atonement. Disregarding this commandment would have resulted in his death:

"The LORD said to Moses: 'Tell your brother Aaron that he shall not enter at any time into the holy place inside the veil, before the mercy seat which is on the ark, or he will die; for I will appear in the cloud over the mercy seat'" (Leviticus 16:2).

According to Leviticus 16, each year on the Day of Atonement, Aaron would...

1. Prepare himself for what lay ahead

2. Purify himself according to God's instructions

3. Clothe himself, first in the ornate, colorful garb of the high priest and then all in white to symbolize humility and purity before God

4. Sacrifice a bull for his own sin and the sin of his household

5. Offer a ram as a burnt offering

6. Select two goats, designating one to be the "scapegoat" that would be released alive into the wilderness bearing the sins of the people, while the other was offered as a burnt offering

7. Anoint the horns and sides of the golden altar of incense in the inner court with blood

8. Take coals and incense from the golden altar, enter the Holy of Holies, and place the incense before the mercy seat as an act of intercession

9. Sprinkle the mercy seat with blood from the bull and the goat, in order to purify them from the people's sins

10. Return to the outer court and lay his hands on the head of the scapegoat, confess the sins of the people over it, and then send it into the wilderness where the goat remained until its death

For as long as the Israelites had a Tabernacle in which to worship or the Temple stood in Jerusalem, these rituals were performed by the high priest on the Day of Atonement year after year.

Let's dig now for the buried treasure God has hidden in the pattern of the high priest and the animal sacrifices.

THE BURIED TREASURE OF THE HIGH PRIEST

Just as Moses was a type of Christ, so do Aaron and the animal sacrifices represent types for how Jesus would one day sacrifice Himself on the

Cross on our behalf and also serve as our high priest. Like Aaron and the animal sacrifices, Jesus…

- Prepared Himself for what lay ahead
- Kept Himself pure before God
- Became for us our sin offering
- Purified the Temple in Heaven with His blood
- Was the "Scapegoat" on whose head our sins were laid

Like Aaron, Jesus was anointed and set apart for His role as high priest (Exodus 28:41; Mark 14:3). Both wore the linen robe of the high priest (Leviticus 16:4; John 19:23) and both bore the 12 tribes of Israel on their breast—Aaron in the *natural* by wearing the priestly ephod as God had commanded (Exodus 28:4) and Jesus in the *spiritual* by bearing our cause before the Father (John 17).

Whenever the Israelites stopped to set up camp as they traveled through the wilderness, Aaron was to establish his personal camp to the east. By doing so, the Israelites high priest was always positioned by the *one* entrance leading into the Tabernacle. This is a picture of how Jesus as our high priest is *the* entrance...the *one* gate...the *only* way by which we can enter into God's presence (John 14:6).

Aaron and Jesus both stood in the gap in intercession on behalf of the people (Leviticus 16:12-13, 16; Hebrews 7:25), and just as Aaron entered the Holy of Holies to cleanse it from the sins of the people with a blood sacrifice (Leviticus 16:14-16), so did Jesus enter the Holy of Holies in the heavenly Tabernacle and purify it with His blood (Hebrews 9:11-12; 23-24).

Even while there are many meaningful similarities between Aaron as the Israelites' high priest and Jesus as our high priest, there is a significant difference.

The blood of the animal sacrifices offered in the outer court to atone for the sins of the people and applied to the mercy seat in the Holy of Holies protected them from God's wrath. But although the blood *covered* the sins of the people, it couldn't permanently wipe away their guilt (Hebrews 10:3-4, 11). Because of this, Aaron and all the priests who followed him had to repeat the same sacrifices and rituals day after day in the outer court and year after year on the Day of Atonement.

However, when Jesus died on the Cross as God's sacrificial Lamb to take away the sins of the whole world, He died *once* for *ALL!*

"Every priest stands daily ministering and offering time after time the same sacrifices, which can never take away sins; but He, having offered one sacrifice for sins for all time, sat down at the right hand of God, waiting from that time onward until His enemies be made a footstool

for His feet. For by one offering He has perfected for all time those who are sanctified" (Hebrews 10:11-14).

There was no longer a need for the Temple sacrifices at the bronze altar or a high priest to go into the Holy of Holies. The highest of all priests had eternally and permanently wiped away the sins of all those who would accept His sacrificial death as the one and only atonement for their sins. His work on the Cross was a finished work.

"IT IS FINISHED!"

One of the most profound and moving types for Christ in the Old Testament lies hidden in the blood sacrifice of the outer court.

After the animal had been slain and placed on the altar, the priest would watch and wait until the offering had been consumed in the fire. Then he would stretch out his arms and cry out "It is finished!"

In the same way, when Jesus was hanging on the Cross with His arms outstretched, He cried out right as He died, *"It is finished!"* The Pharisees, Sadducees, and maybe even the high priest Caiaphas who witnessed this powerful moment surely would have understood the significance of Jesus' last words.

Perhaps there were those at Jesus' crucifixion who also were at the Jordan River when the crowds had come to John to be baptized. With His last breath, Jesus clearly identified Himself with the sin offerings sacrificed on the bronze altar, fulfilling John's prophetic words when he pointed to Jesus

"For by one offering He has perfected for all time those who are sanctified."

and declared, *"Behold, the Lamb of God who takes away the sin of the world!"* (John 1:29).

At the precise moment that Jesus hung His head and died, an amazing miracle occurred in the Temple, to which both Matthew and Mark testify: *"The veil of the temple was torn in two from top to bottom"* (Matthew 27:51; Mark 17:38).

Why was this torn veil a miracle, and what significance does it have for us today? Let's dig a little deeper to discover some more buried treasure....

THE VEIL IS TORN

There were two veils used in Moses' wilderness Tabernacle—the outer veil, or the first veil, which served as the doorway leading from the outer court into the inner court, and then there was the inner veil, or the second veil, which separated the inner court from the Holy of Holies. This is the veil that was torn when Jesus died, and the description for it is found in Exodus 26:31-33:

"You shall make a veil of blue and purple and scarlet material and fine twisted linen; it shall be made with cherubim, the work of a skillful workman.

"You shall hang it on four pillars of acacia overlaid with gold, their hooks also being of gold, on four sockets of silver.

"You shall hang up the veil under the clasps, and shall bring in the ark of the testimony there within the veil; and the veil shall serve for you as a partition between the holy place and the holy of holies."

By the time the Tabernacle had been replaced with the Temple in Jerusalem as the center of Jewish worship, the construction of the veil had evolved into an amazing process described in the *Mishnah*, the written tradition of Jewish rabbinical law.

I had always pictured the Temple veil as having been made from a flimsy, lacy or gauzy kind of material, but boy was I wrong! According to rabbinical teaching, the veil was 60 feet high, 30 feet wide, and *a hands breadth thick* (between 4 and 6 inches)! In order to determine if a veil was of a high enough quality for use in the Temple, it would be hooked up to two teams of oxen pulling in opposite directions in an attempt to tear it apart. Only those veils which withstood this extreme test were used.

So the Temple veil had survived this endurance test, yet it still was torn from top to bottom at the moment of Jesus' death. Unbelievable!

In addition, the veil was torn from top to bottom, and even if by some form of superhuman strength the priests *possibly* could have torn it in two, it would have been impossible for them to have reached up 60 feet to tear it from the top. Only *GOD* could perform such a miracle! What does this mean, and why did God do this?

Hebrews 10:19-22 provides us with the answer:

"Therefore, brethren, since we have confidence to enter the holy place by the blood of Jesus, by a new and living way which He inaugurated for us through the veil, that is, His flesh, and since we have a great priest over the house of God,

"Let us draw near with a sincere heart in full assurance of faith, having our hearts sprinkled clean from an evil conscience and our bodies washed with pure water."

Just as Jesus' flesh was torn to make a pathway for us into God's presence, so did God supernaturally tear the veil that separated us from the Holy of Holies so that we could draw near to Him in faith.

Now, I want us to pause for a moment and read a very unusual verse in the New Testament. The writer of Hebrews tell us that…

"Behind the second veil there was a tabernacle which is called the Holy of Holies, having a golden altar of incense, and the Ark of the Covenant covered on all sides with gold, in which was a golden jar holding the manna, and Aaron's rod which budded, and table of the Covenant, and above it were the cherubim of glory overshadowing the mercy seat; but of these things we cannot now speak in detail" (Hebrews 9:3-5).

When I read these verses, I said to myself, "Wait a minute! That's not right! The altar of incense was in the *inner* court. How in the world did it get moved into the Holy of Holies?"

Well, I don't know the answer to this question for sure, but I *do* know that *"God is not a man that He should lie"* (Numbers 23:19). So if the Word says that the golden altar of incense in the Temple was now in the Holy of Holies, then it must be true.

I believe that when Jesus said, *"It is finished"* and the veil separating the inner court from the Holy of Holies was torn in two, God supernaturally moved the altar of incense into the Holy of Holies. By doing so, He would have revealed yet another pattern to us: It's our worship, offered freely from the depths of our heart and out of our brokenness and crushing that brings us into God's presence.

By His death on the Cross, our high priest Jesus paid the highest price to allow us access to the very Holy of Holies. God *Himself* tore the veil to demonstrate that His blood requirement for the remission of our sins had been forever satisfied through His Son's sacrificial death.

No longer must we be separated from an intimate relationship with Him. Instead of being terrified of God striking us dead for entering the Holy of Holies in an unworthy manner, He lovingly invites us to freely and boldly enter into His presence with confidence based on the atoning work of Jesus Christ.

Will you accept His invitation?

DIGGING DEEPER

1. Based on what you now understand about "types" in Scripture, make a list of the ways that the animal sacrifices were a type, or a pattern, of Jesus as our sacrifice.

2. Hebrews 10:14 tells us that, *"For by one offering He has perfected for all time those who are sanctified."* This means that if Jesus Christ is your Lord, then *YOU* have been *"perfected for all time."* Does how you think about yourself reflect this truth? Why or why not?

3. Reread Hebrews 10:19-22 where God invites you to boldly enter into the intimacy of His presence. Describe how you feel when you think about entering into the "Holy of Holies." Are you bold? Fearful? Unsure? Thrilled? Intimidated? Eager? Ashamed?

4. Spend time telling the Lord how you feel about coming into His presence and being in an intimate relationship with Him. Ask Him to help you feel His deep love for you drawing you closer to Himself.

CHAPTER 17

In His Presence

"Therefore, brethren, since we have confidence to enter

the holy place by the blood of Jesus,

by a new and living way... let us draw near with

a sincere heart in full assurance of faith."

HEBREWS 10:19, 20, 22

*T*HE PATHWAY ON WHICH WE'VE been journeying together has led us beyond the veil and into the most holy of all places...the very presence of God. Our desire to know Him and be known by Him has brought us to this moment.

As I shared with you in the first chapter, my own journey began years ago when I was desperately hungry to experience a deeper intimacy in my relationship with the Lord. I wasn't content with where I was in my walk with Him. I knew there was *more,* and I was determined to passionately pursue Him with abandonment.

That morning in the hotel coffee shop, the Lord spoke these five words to my spirit:

"REPENT. PRAISE. WORSHIP. OFFERING. SACRIFICE."

Together, you and I have searched out some of the vital pictures, patterns, and mysteries God has hidden in His Word. We've discovered how the outer court of the Tabernacle was a place of *REPENTANCE.* We've unearthed the treasure of *PRAISE* in the Stairs of Ascent, and we've mined the "gold" of *WORSHIP* in the inner court as God chose to reveal them through the golden lampstand, the table of showbread, and the golden altar of incense.

And now it's time for us to explore the mystery of the Holy of Holies and how this is the ultimate place of *OFFERING* and *SACRIFICE.*

THE HOLY OF HOLIES

The Holy of Holies in the wilderness Tabernacle was a room with dimensions that formed a perfect cube: 10 cubits long by 10 cubits wide by 10 cubits high (15 feet x 15 feet x 15 feet). (Note: It's interesting to consider this "cube" where the presence of God dwelt on earth and contrast that to the description of Heaven in Revelation 21:16. Revelation describes the city of God laid out as a cube in three dimensions, meaning its length and width are equal to its height.

During the 40 years that the Israelites were in the wilderness, the presence of God hovered over the Holy of Holies in the form of a pillar of fire by night and a cloud by day (Numbers 9:15-23).

This holiest of all rooms contained only one piece of furniture at the time: the Ark of the Covenant. When God gave Moses the instructions regarding its construction, He said He would *MEET* with His people and *SPEAK* to His people before the Ark of the Covenant and tell them what to do.

*"There I will **meet** with you; and from above the mercy seat, from between the two cherubim which are upon the ark of the testimony, I will **speak** to you about all that I will give you in **commandment** for the sons of Israel"* (Exodus 25:22).

Exodus 25:10-22 describes the Ark in great detail. It was...

- A box, 3 feet 9 inches long x 2 feet 3 inches wide x 2 feet 3 inches high
- Made of acacia wood
- Overlaid with pure gold inside and out, with a gold molding all the way around
- Fitted with gold rings on the four corners to hold the acacia wood poles (also overlaid with gold) used for transporting it

The lid of the Ark was 3 feet 9 inches long x 2 feet 3 inches wide. Called the "Mercy Seat," the entire lid was made of pure gold and served as the Throne for God's presence. On either end were two cherubim (worshipping angels) made of hammered gold that sat facing each other with their outstretched wings covering the Mercy Seat.

According to God's commandments, the Ark contained three items that were to serve as constant reminders of the Israelites' frailty and dependence on God, and His abiding faithfulness to His Covenant people:

- The pot of manna (Exodus 16:33)
- The tablets with the Ten Commandments (Exodus 25:16; 34:29)
- Aaron's rod that had budded (Numbers 17:1-10)

As I shared with you in the previous chapter, once a year on the Day of Atonement, the high priest would enter the Holy of Holies to offer incense up to God and sprinkle the blood from the sacrifices on the Mercy Seat to purify it from the people's sins.

The desire of God's heart always has been to draw His children into increasingly deeper levels of intimacy with Him. He provided Moses with a detailed description of the Holy of Holies for two reasons:

1) to convey His demands for holiness and 2) to reveal the pattern for experiencing the rich rewards of intimacy with Him.

Let's dig now for the treasure God has buried in this most holy place.

WE ARE THE 'OFFERING'

Because God provided Moses with clear directions for the Holy of Holies and the Ark of the Covenant, it's clear that He *wants* to meet with us, speak to us and give us commandment (show us what to do) in this place of stillness and intimacy.

*"And there will I **meet** with you; and from above the mercy seat, from between the two cherubim which are upon the ark of the testimony, I will **speak** to you about all that I will give you in **commandment** for the sons of Israel"* (Exodus 25:22).

Throughout Scripture, God invites us to draw near to Him and be with Him:

"The LORD is near to all who call upon Him, to all who call upon Him in truth" (Psalm 145:18).

"I have loved you with an everlasting love; therefore I have drawn you with lovingkindness" (Jeremiah 31:3).

"Draw near to God and He will draw near to you" (James 4:8).

But through the centuries, God's standard for holiness has never changed, and even as He invites us to know Him intimately, He still requires "blood" and "incense" for us to enter His presence and be with Him.

Just as the high priest brought the coals and incense from the golden altar into the Holy of Holies, so must each one of us serve as the priest of our own "temple," entering into God's holy presence bearing the sweet-smelling incense of our worship. And just as the high priest anointed the Mercy Seat with the blood of the animal sacrifice to cleanse it from the sins of the people, so must we enter the Holy of Holies anointed with the cleansing blood of the Lord Jesus Christ.

Unless we maintain a posture of worship and humility before Him,

Unless we maintain a

posture of worship and

humility before Him,

entering His presence

is impossible.

entering His presence is impossible. Without the sacrificial blood of Jesus covering us, we *cannot* come into the Holy of Holies because His holiness is too magnificent and our sinfulness too great.

When we enter into the holiness of God's presence, we're entering a place of *OFFERING*. In the outer court, one way we draw near to God is to bring God our tithes and offerings and receive the offering *JESUS* made on our behalf. However, within the Holy of Holies, *WE* become the offering as we humbly submit our lives in an intimate relationship with our loving God.

In many ways, intimacy with the Lord is like the intimate relationship between a husband and a wife.

TRUE INTIMACY

When a husband and a wife have a relationship solidly built on a foundation of love, trust, and mutual respect, the closeness of their relationship is reflected in the most intimate moments of their marriage. In the Bible, the word used to describe this is the Hebrew word *yada'* meaning "to know, perceive, recognize, to know intimately."

Yada' is used when Scripture says that Adam *"knew"* his wife Eve (Genesis 4:1), and Elkannah *"knew"* his wife Hannah (1 Samuel 1:19).

This is the kind of love relationship God desires to have with each one of us—a relationship characterized by true knowledge and intimacy—and when He says, *"Before I formed you in the womb I* **knew** *you, and before you were born I consecrated you"* (Jeremiah 1:5), it's this same word *yada'* that He uses.

God revealed a pattern for intimacy with Him in Ephesians 5:28-32 when Paul describes the mystery of the marriage relationship:

"So husbands ought also to love their own wives as their own bodies. He who loves his own wife loves himself; for no one ever hated his own flesh, but nourishes and cherishes it, just as Christ also does the church, because we are members of His body.

*"For this reason a man shall leave his father and mother and shall be joined to his wife, and the two shall become one flesh. **This***

mystery is great; but I am speaking with reference to Christ and the church."

When a husband and wife truly "know" one another, they aren't just aware of their spouse's favorite color, the restaurant where he or she likes to eat, or even special secrets that they confide to no one else except one another. For a man and a woman to be truly intimate, they must know and experience intimacy with one another on *every* level of their relationship...emotionally, mentally, and physically.

The sad thing is that so many of us have a false sense of intimacy about our marriage. As husbands and wives, it's easy to think that because we watch TV together, talk about the kids, make vacation plans, or enjoy the marriage bed occasionally, we have an intimate relationship with our spouse. But this simply isn't so. There is a difference between companionship and intimacy. For there to be *true* intimacy in marriage, a husband and wife must...

- Honor their covenant to one another by "leaving and cleaving"
- Be eternally faithful to each other
- Devote special attention to one another
- Spend meaningful time together
- Prefer the other's needs above their own
- Share the thoughts and feelings of their innermost being
- Offer themselves to one another in times of intimate, selfless abandonment
- Experience the joy of being fully known as they lovingly "lose themselves" in one another.

It's the same way in our relationship with God: Many of us also have a false sense of intimacy with Him. It's easy to believe that because we go to church, talk to Him, read the Word, serve Him faithfully, and even experience great times of praise and worship, we know Him intimately. But much more is required than this to have an intimate relationship with God. There's a difference between knowing *about* God and *knowing* God.

"But you, when you pray, go into your inner room, close your door and pray to your Father who is in secret, and your Father who sees what is done in secret will reward you."

In Chapter 4, I shared how God wants us to bring Him our *ALL*. However, our *ALL* isn't just our time, treasure, and talents. In the Holy of Holies, we offer *ourselves* to the Lord without distraction. We offer our very being to Him with abandonment. In the Holy of Holies, we lose ourselves in the magnitude of His deep and abiding love for us. In the stillness of this place, we are fully known and experience true intimacy with the Lord.

But the offering of ourselves to God requires **SACRIFICE.**

DYING DAILY

In the outer court, *JESUS* was the sacrifice, having suffered both horrifying physical pain and even worse, the unimaginable pain of having His Heavenly Father turn away from Him while He was on the Cross as the sin of the entire world covered Him. But in the Holy of Holies, *WE* are the sacrifice.

In the Holy of Holies, we offer ourselves by sacrificing the only thing we really have to give Him: our very lives. As we come into His presence to be alone with Him in intimate times of worship, we *"die daily"* (1 Corinthians 15:31).

Hundreds of priests served God by fulfilling their duties in the outer court of the Temple…but only one priest went into the Holy of Holies. In the outer and inner courts, the high priest ministered on behalf of the people, but in the Holy of Holies, he ministered to *God.*

In the same way, in the outer court—and even

in the inner court—of our spiritual journey with the Lord, we use our time, talent, and treasure to serve the Lord by serving His people and winning lost Souls to Christ for God's Kingdom. However, when I go into the Holy of Holies, I go in *alone*. In the very presence of the Lord, there is no room for anyone or anything except Him and me.

We too easily confuse ministry activity with intimacy. We can be so busy doing things *for* God that we're too busy to spend time *with* Him. I believe that, sadly, most of us spend our lives serving the Lord as outer court priests. But this isn't what He desires for us. God loves us so much that He wants to be alone with us in a place of intimacy. He calls each of us to join Him in the hidden place of the Holy of Holies, where no one sees us, and no one can flatter us for all our hard work.

"But you, when you pray, go into your inner room, close your door and pray to your Father who is in secret, and your Father who sees what is done in secret will reward you" (Matthew 6:6).

As we sacrifice our busyness and the empty words of other's opinions in order to enter into the secret place of the Holy of Holies, our Heavenly Father will be glorified and we will be blessed with the rich reward of an intimate relationship with Him.

NO SWEAT!

In Ezekiel's vision of the Temple, God reveals through the priests and their clothing yet another pattern of what He requires of us who desire intimacy with Him:

"They shall come near to My table to minister to Me and keep My charge.

"It shall be that when they enter at the gates of the inner court, they shall be clothed with linen garments; and wool shall not be on them while they are ministering in the gates of the inner court and in the house.

*"Linen turbans shall be on their heads and linen undergarments shall be on their loins; **they shall not gird themselves with anything which makes them sweat**"* (Ezekiel 44:16-18).

God said that the priests would come near to *"minister"* to Him.

The word "minister" is a Hebrew word *sharath,* which means "to attend as a servant or worshipper; to serve or wait on." Like the Temple priests, God desires for us to serve Him in quiet times of waiting on Him in worship.

Why did God command the priests who went into the Holy of Holies to wear linen and to wear nothing made from wool? Because He didn't want them to sweat!

Sweat represents our flesh and striving under own strength to "make things happen." God never anoints the work of our flesh, and there is no place for it in the Holy of Holies. God is Spirit, and we must worship Him in spirit and in truth, not in flesh and the self-deception of our own strength (John 4:24). Those works that we produce as a result of our own "sweat" will amount to nothing but wood, hay, and straw.

"For no man can lay a foundation other than the one which is laid, which is Jesus Christ.

"Now if any man builds on the foundation with gold, silver, precious stones, wood, hay, straw, each man's work will become evident; for the day will show it because it is to be revealed with fire, and the fire itself will test the quality of each man's work.

"If any man's work which he has built on it remains, he will receive a reward" (1 Corinthians 3:11-14).

As Believers, we're too well-acquainted with trying to produce great things for God by the sweat of our brow. For this reason, refusing to strive to is one of the greatest sacrifices we can make as we move into increasingly deeper levels of relationship with the Lord.

Deep within our spirit resides the Holy of Holies, the place where God waits for us to offer ourselves to Him in worship. All the things we *DO* for Him in ministry are worthless compared to the sacrifice of humility and brokenness before Him:

"For You do not delight in sacrifice, otherwise I would give it; You are not pleased with burnt offering. The sacrifices of God are a broken spirit; a broken and a contrite heart, O God, You will not despise" (Psalm 51:16-17).

While our worshipful times of intimacy with the Lord may include Scripture, singing, and prayer, sometimes He simply wants us to offer to Him the sacrifice of our busyness, works, and sweat, and instead just *BE* with Him in quietness, stillness, and silence:

"In repentance and rest you will be saved, in quietness and trust is your strength" (Isaiah 30:15).

"The LORD is good to those who wait for Him, to the person who seeks Him. It is good that he waits silently for the salvation of the LORD" (Lamentations 3:25-26).

THE POWER OF TRANSFORMATION

So often what motivates us to have a relationship with God is our need. We may go through the motions of worship, but if we're honest, the *real* cry of our heart is "Gimme this God," or "I need that Lord." This isn't relationship, and it's certainly not intimacy. The truth is that although God loves us and is heartbroken over our desperate neediness, He doesn't respond to our need: He responds to our faith-filled, loving, obedience and the intimacy of our relationship with Him.

When my grandkids call me at the office, I don't care what I'm doing, what meeting I'm in, or who I'm talking to. My assistant knows to put that call through to me right away. Why? Because of the intimate relationship I have with them.

The same is true of our relationship with God. He isn't some far off, distant God who wants to hide Himself from His children. No, God is a God who is near to us: *"'Am I a God who is near,' declares the LORD, 'And not a God afar off?'"* (Jeremiah 23:23)

My heart is crying out for *more* of God... *more* of His presence, *more* intimacy, *more* relationship, *more* power. But power can only come through transformation, and transformation only comes through intimacy with Him. Intimacy is birthed from relationship, and relationship is the result of spending time in His presence.

The only way we will have a powerful spiritual life is by spending time in God's presence. Transformation is a process...a pattern...one building block resting upon another.

When we...

- Offer ourselves to Him in abandonment
- Die daily
- Sacrifice our striving and simply come to Him in brokenness
- Seek to be alone with Him in intimate times of worship

...then He responds to the cries of our heart: *"Call to Me and I will answer you, and I will tell you great and mighty things, which you do not know"* (Jeremiah 33:3).

As we wait on the Lord and give ourselves as an **OFFERING** and a **SACRIFICE** to Him in times of worship, He responds to the cries of our heart and blesses us:

"Therefore the LORD longs to be gracious to you, and therefore He waits on high to have compassion on you. For the LORD is a God of justice; how blessed are all those who long for Him.

"O people in Zion, inhabitant in Jerusalem, you will weep no longer. He will surely be gracious to you at the sound of your cry; when He hears it, He will answer you" (Isaiah 30:18-19).

The desire of God's heart is to *MEET* with us and *SPEAK* to us in the intimacy of the Holy of Holies. Will you choose to meet Him there?

DIGGING DEEPER

1. According to Exodus 25:22, God wants you to draw near to Him in worship so that He can meet with you and speak to you. Are you eager to do this? Why or why not?

2. Paul uses the analogy of the marriage relationship to describe the intimate relationship the Lord wants to have with you. Are you comfortable with this comparison? Why or why not?

3. God makes it clear that there is to be no "sweating" in His presence. Which description best fits you and where you are right now in your relationship with the Lord?

   • "I am working very hard for the Lord and His Kingdom, and so I tend to be busy, overworked, stressed, and tired."
   • "I am spending lots of time worshipping the Lord, ministering to Him, and just being with Him in quietness, stillness, and silence."

4. Spend time with the Lord. Read Hebrews 10:18-22. Trust that because of Jesus' blood, you can enter into the Holy of Holies and draw near to God in faith. Receive His amazing love and His 100% acceptance of you as His child. Tell Him how much you love Him and desire to go deeper in an intimate relationship with Him. Worship Him in stillness. Wait on Him. Listen for what He wants to say to you in the silence.

CHAPTER 18

Thirty...Sixty... OR One Hundredfold?

"...and others fell on good soil and yielded a crop,

some a hundredfold, some sixty, and some thirty.

He who has ears to hear, let him hear."

MATTHEW 13: 8-9

*Y*OU AND I WERE CREATED to worship God. The mystery He has revealed through the wilderness Tabernacle and Solomon's Temple...the outer court with the bronze altar and the bronze laver...the inner court with the golden lampstand, table of showbread, and golden altar of incense...the Holy of Holies and the Ark of the Covenant...is the pathway leading to His glorious presence.

Only in God's presence do we...

- Experience His tender love
- Find hope and healing
- Know the peace that surpasses all understanding
- Discover true freedom
- Receive the rich rewards that can only come from an intimate relationship with Him

But if this is true—and I assure you, it *IS* true—why do so few of us complete the journey? Why do we resist exploring the pictures, patterns and mysteries of His Word to find the gold He has buried there for us to discover? Why aren't we pursuing God with all of our heart, soul, mind, and strength?

I believe that while many of us truly desire a more intimate relationship with God, we're unwilling to pay the price to enter the Holy of Holies. Most of us like the *idea* of being intimate with the Lord, but when it comes right down to it, we can't—or won't—respond to the five words God spoke to my spirit:

REPENT.

PRAISE.

WORSHIP.

OFFERING.

SACRIFICE.

"REPENT. PRAISE. WORSHIP. OFFERING. SACRIFICE."

God's desire is to welcome you into His presence and surround you with His love and mercy. He longs for you to receive all the blessings that intimacy with Him brings. My friend, this is why He has led me to write this book: to help you pursue the pathway to His presence and know the joy of intimacy with Him.

In order to help you move deeper into an intimate relationship with Him, let's look at some of the barriers that could be preventing you from moving from the outer court, through the inner court, and into the Holy of Holies.

BARRIERS TO INTIMACY

1. Fear

Fear of *God*: Many of us are *afraid* to enter into God's presence. Either because of our upbringing or erroneous teaching in the Church, we falsely believe that God is a disapproving Father or an angry Judge. Although we may be comfortable with Jesus as our loving Savior and relate well with Him, time alone with the Heavenly Father must be avoided at all costs so as not to experience what we fear will be displeasure.

Fear of *Intimacy*: Others of us are actually afraid of intimacy. Experience has taught us that intimate relationships are painful and not worth the hurt that is sure to follow if we pursue the pathway to God's presence.

2. Guilt

Some of us won't dare to enter God's presence because we're living in willful disobedience to His Word. Like Adam and Eve, in our sinfulness we run *away* from God rather than running *to* Him for forgiveness and restoration. Because of our deliberate rebellion, our sin blocks us from experiencing intimacy with Him.

3. Shame

Others of us are so crippled with shame that we see ourselves as unworthy to be in God's presence. We're ashamed—not necessarily because of any sin we've committed—but because of the unworthiness that engulfs who we essentially *are*. Our very identity is one of shame, and because of this, we simply can't believe that God would even *want* to have an intimate relationship with us.

4. Doubt and Hopelessness

Because of seeds the enemy has sown in our minds, we doubt that God's Word is true...His love for us is real...He really *is* good...or that He will fulfill His promises to us. Our skepticism holds us back from pursuing Him passionately. Doubt inevitably leads to hopelessness, and hopelessness suffocates and deadens our desire for intimacy.

5. Apathy

Some of us are apathetic. Maybe we've tried the "intimacy thing" with God before and found it just didn't work for us. Perhaps we've worked hard to enter His presence, and we're tired of trying. Over time, we've given up pursuing Him, and now we just don't care anymore.

6. Offense

Many in the Body of Christ have been wounded by family, friends, coworkers, bosses, church members, and ministry leadership. Because we've failed to truly forgive those who have deeply hurt us, our unforgiveness has turned into bitterness. And as God warns in Scripture, when we refuse to forgive others, we're unable to receive His forgiveness (Mark 11:26). Without forgiveness, we can't experience times of intimacy in His presence.

7. Unfaithfulness

Just as in a marriage when one spouse is unfaithful to the marriage covenant and the relationship is strained and damaged, when we're unfaithful to the Lord, our relationship with Him is negatively impacted. Our unfaithfulness is the result of loving the things of this world and pursuing the lusts of our flesh more than loving Him and passionately pursuing the pathway leading to His presence (1 John 1:15-17).

8. Selfishness

There are those of us who aren't pursuing intimacy with God simply because we don't *want* to. We refuse to give up our worldly pleasures because the enemy has deceived us into believing that the "boring" things God wants to give us can't compare to the exciting things the world has to offer. Rather than Jesus being our Lord, *we* are seated on the throne of our life, and we have no intentions of moving off of it.

9. Insensitivity

Pursuing the things of this world and following after other

lovers (Hosea 2:5-6) instead of pursuing God and intimacy with Him eventually results in our hearts becoming darkened and calloused to Him and His ways (Ephesians 5:17-24). Our spirit becomes insensitive to His voice and the moving of His Holy Spirit, and so intimacy with Him is impossible.

10. Busyness

An overwhelming number of us are just too busy to pursue an intimate relationship with God. As with a husband and a wife, intimacy takes *TIME*, but time feels like such a rare commodity. Sure, it would be great to hang out in the Holy of Holies, but when we're sitting before the Lord in silence and worshipping Him, other "important" things just aren't getting done.

The truth is that all of these barriers prevent us from ministering before the Lord in the Holy of Holies. We can't serve Him from a distance, and we can't receive the fullness of His love if we choose to hang out for the rest of our lives in the outer court, or even the inner court.

God invites each of us to enter in and experience the rich rewards that intimacy with Him brings. However, He's not going to force us into an intimate relationship with Him. He won't hunt us down in the outer court, and He will never drag us kicking and screaming from the inner court into the fullness of His presence.

What He *does* do is extend the invitation and then patiently and lovingly wait for us to accept it. The choice is ours.

THIRTY, SIXTY, OR ONE HUNDREDFOLD

If you've been a Believer for any length of time, you probably know the parable of the seed sower:

"Listen to this! Behold, the sower went out to sow; as he was sowing, some seed fell beside the road, and the birds came and ate it up.

"Other seed fell on the rocky ground where it did not have much

soil; and immediately it sprang up because it had no depth of soil. And after the sun had risen, it was scorched; and because it had no root, it withered away.

"Other seed fell among the thorns, and the thorns came up and choked it, and it yielded no crop. Other seeds fell into the good soil, and as they grew up and increased, they yielded a crop and produced thirty, sixty, and a hundredfold" (Mark 4:3-9).

Notice that *all* the seed that fell onto good soil yielded a crop, but not all of the crops were of the same value: some produced 30 times the amount of seeds planted, others resulted in a 60 times the amount of seeds sown, and then some seeds reaped a *100-fold* Harvest!

That's a 30...60...*or* a 100-fold return on the seed sower's investment. I don't know about you, but I would much rather receive 100 times what I sowed than 30!

In addition to the many hidden treasures in this parable about evangelism, the necessity of Sowing financial Seeds into Good Ground, and how the enemy seeks to devour God's Seed, I also believe there's another pattern God wants us to discover in this story of the 30, 60, or 100-fold crop.

BODY, SOUL, AND SPIRIT

Genesis 2:7 says, *"Then the LORD God formed man of dust from the ground, and breathed into his nostrils the breath of life; and man became a living being."* There are three important things to note in this short verse:

1. **God formed man from the dust of the ground.**
2. **God breathed the breath of life into him.**
3. **Man became a living being.**

God's spirit gave man his body, his soul, and his spirit.

Then in 1 Thessalonians 5:23, Paul writes, *"Now may the God of peace Himself sanctify you entirely; and may your spirit and soul and body be preserved complete, without blame at the coming of our Lord Jesus Christ."* Note that Paul names three aspects that comprise who we are: our body, our soul, and our spirit.

Our **body** is our physical self that houses our soul and spirit. It's our "earth suit" (someday, we'll live in new, resurrected bodies in Heaven!) and represents the outer court, which is a picture of a *30-fold* relationship with the Lord. In the outer court, we accept Jesus as our Savior and are baptized by the water and the Word. This is an essential beginning, but we can't stop there.

Our **soul** is made up of our mind, will, and emotions. It's the part of us that says, "I think," "I will," and "I feel." Our soul influences our body and represents the inner court, which is a picture of a 60-fold relationship with the Lord. In the inner court, we're illuminated by God's Word, and our understanding of Jesus as the Light of the world deepens. We feast on Him—the Bread of Life—and we enjoy of fresh manna as we read the Word daily and as we partake in communion.

In the inner court, our spiritual life deepens as we communicate with God through the illumination of His Word, as we pray, worship Him, and allow Him to crush us into a sweet incense that arises before Him. Although our understanding of God and experience with Him in the inner court is awesome, it is not the full expression of an intimate relationship with Him. There is *more!*

Our **spirit** is the part of us that is made in God's image. When we accept Jesus Christ as our Lord and Savior, it's our spirit that's instantly justified

"Now may the

God of peace

Himself sanctify

you entirely; and

may your spirit

and soul and

body be preserved

complete, without

blame at the

coming of our

Lord Jesus Christ."

by His blood, and it's on our spirit that God places the seal of His Holy Spirit (Ephesians 1:13). Our spirit influences our soul, and represents the Holy of Holies, which is a picture of the 100-fold relationship and experience with the Lord. In this holy place, we're rewarded with His presence, peace, and power. We sense His overwhelming love for us, and our spirit becomes one with His.

I also want to point out to you that in the outer court, the sun and the moon provided *natural* light. In the inner court, the light source was candlelight, which was *manmade,* and in the Holy of Holies, the light source was *supernatural,* because it was the *shekinah* glory of God Himself that shone in the darkness. From this we see yet another pattern of the progression of our intimate relationship with God.

ONE SPIRIT

When Adam and Eve sinned in the garden, their *spirits* were cut off from God, and they became *"dead in trespasses and sins"* (Ephesians 2:1). The consequence of their sin is that our body will decay and eventually die forever. However, our soul—our mind, will, and emotions—and the choices we make will determine where our spirit (housed in a new body) will spend eternity.

Intimacy between God and us could only be restored through the sacrifice of His Son on the Cross. Just as the bronze altar was the first piece of furniture encountered by the priests in the outer court, so is Jesus the first step we must take on the pathway to God's presence. Like the animal sacrifices in the outer court, only through Jesus' shed blood do we receive forgiveness for our sins.

It's vital to understand that only our spirit—not our soul and not our body—is capable of direct fellowship with God. As I shared with you in the previous chapter, God is a *Spirit,* and those who want intimacy with Him must worship Him in spirit and in truth (John 4:24). When we accept Jesus' sacrifice made on our behalf as the payment for our sins, it's our **spirit** that's saved, renewed and restored to fellowship with God.

It's vital to understand

that only our spirit—not

our soul and not our

body—is capable of direct

fellowship with God.

Paul wrote to the Corinthians, *"Don't you know that the one who joins himself to a prostitute is one body with her? For He says, 'The two shall become one flesh.' But the one who joins himself to the Lord is one spirit with Him"* (1 Corinthians 6:16-18).

On the one hand, Paul was warning Believers against immorality when he told them to be careful not to be sexually impure. On the other hand, Paul also was making it clear that when we join our spirit with God's spirit, we become one with Him.

When we worship, God intends for all three parts of us to be engaged: body, soul, and spirit. But it's our **spirit** that is one with His, and an intimate relationship is the result. Our body and soul simply aren't capable of this kind of intimacy with the Lord. Only our spirit can have union with God, and this union comes through worship!

MORE

Some days I feel as though I take a step or two forward on the pathway leading to a deepening intimacy with God, and then there are those days when I seem to take a giant step *backward.* Regardless, I am DETERMINED not to live in a 30-fold relationship with Him.

I don't want to settle for an outer court experience with Him. Yes, I'm grateful I've been saved by the blood of the Lamb at the bronze altar, and yes, I'm glad I've been baptized and washed by the water and the Word at the bronze laver. But this isn't enough for me, and I hope it's not enough for you either.

To be completely honest, I have to admit I've spent most of my life living in the inner court and being satisfied with a 60-fold relationship with the Lord. And the inner court life *is* wonderful. I've experienced God through the golden lampstand and the illumination of His Word. I've feasted on Jesus as my daily bread at the table of showbread and conformed my will to His, and I've offered up my worship and intercession to God at the golden altar, even in the midst of times when I felt like I was being crushed by His mortar and pestle.

But in these last years, God has graciously led me on the pathway to His presence, and so I'm no longer content with a 60-fold relationship in the inner court. I have experienced firsthand the true intimacy that is only found in the Holy of Holies. I've met with Him there. I've offered Him my very life as a living sacrifice.

And as I've ministered to Him in this holy place, He's spoken to me. I've experienced the reality of His presence, peace, and power. I've been enveloped by His love and overwhelmed by His mercy and grace, and I will never again be satisfied with anything less than a 100-fold relationship.

How about you? Do you want *more?* More of His presence in your life? More of His peace? More of His power? More intimacy with Him? *MORE?*

As you read this book right now, is your spirit resounding with a thundering, "YES!"? Are you feeling a stirring deep within...a longing for *more*...a desire to enter into the intimacy of the Holy of Holies...a hunger to taste for yourself and see that the Lord is *good?* Or maybe you're wondering if a 100-fold relationship is even possible: You want what I'm describing, but you're afraid.

Regardless of where you find yourself on this journey, this is a decision each of us must make for ourselves: *"Multitudes, multitudes in the valley of decision. For the day of the LORD is near in the valley of decision"* (Joel 3:14).

HOW FAR DO YOU WANT TO GO?

Know that wherever you are on your journey, God loves you right where you are. He's not impatient with you. He's not frustrated with you. He's not disappointed with you. But He desperately wants you to join Him in the Holy of Holies. He desires you to be in an intimate, 100-fold relationship with Him. He wants to give you *MORE.*

But in order to have more of Him, you'll need to decide how far you want to go. Jesus said, *"Blessed are those who hunger and thirst for righteousness, for they shall be satisfied"* (Matthew 5:6). The Greek word used here for "hunger" is *peinao,* which means "to be famished; to crave."

Imagine you are starving to death and walk into a restaurant filled with buffet tables covered with food. What would you do? Would you mind your manners and patiently wait your turn in line? Would you carefully use all the right silverware, wipe your mouth with your napkin after each bite, and make sure to chew with your mouth closed? I don't think so. A starving person has no manners. I bet you would run over to those tables and begin feasting ravenously on everything in sight.

In the same way, God wants us to *crave* being in His presence. However, so many ministry leaders are focused on politically correct church behavior. They've taught us to sit quietly with our hands folded, or *maybe* even raise our hands in the air a little if an especially powerful praise song is sung.

Sadly, so many of us don't even know we're hungry. We're not starving for God's presence because we haven't experienced true intimacy with Him. In fact, we really don't know what this even means, and so we don't know what we're missing. Instead, we're gorging on a steady diet of "junk food" that disguises just how spiritually malnourished we are.

Are you content with being an acquaintance of the Lord's, or are you starving to know Him intimately? Are you just fine with being good friends, or are you famished for His presence? Will you take the next step along the pathway to His presence, or do you prefer to stay right where you are?

If you're willing to abandon yourself to Him as a living sacrifice... and if you're ready—by His grace and with His strength—to overcome the barriers holding you back from an intimate relationship with Him, then it's time for you to press in...

DIGGING DEEPER

1. At the beginning of this chapter, there is a list of barriers to intimacy with the Lord. Review that list and pick two of the barriers that are especially challenging for you to overcome. Why are these difficult for you?

2. Consider your current relationship with the Lord. Would you describe yourself as having a 30-fold, 60-fold, or 100-fold relationship with Him? Why? Are you satisfied with where you are, or are you hungry for more?

3. Are you content with being an acquaintance of the Lord's, or are you starving to know Him intimately? Why or why not?

4. Spend time with the Lord right now. Share with Him all of your responses from questions 1 through 3. If you're ready to press in, tell Him so, and ask for His grace and strength to help you overcome every barrier.

CHAPTER 19

Press In!

"...that I may know Him and the

power of His resurrection..."

PHILIPPIANS 3:10

*W*ELL MY FRIEND, WE'VE traveled far together along this pathway leading to God's presence. We began at the gates of Solomon's Temple and ended our journey in the Holy of Holies. We've learned much along the way as we explored different pictures and patterns, and we've dug deep for God's hidden treasure buried in the mysteries of His Word.

When Jesus said to the Pharisees, *"For if you believed Moses, you would believe Me, for he wrote about Me"* (John 5:46), He spoke correctly. Moses diligently recorded the clear instructions God gave him regarding the construction of the Tabernacle, its contents, and their placement within the Tabernacle, all the while unaware that he was detailing a prophetic picture of the sacrificial death of the coming Messiah.

I'll invite you to pause for a moment now and form a mental picture of the physical Tabernacle. Imagine the contents of the outer court, the inner court, and the Holy of Holies. With your mind's eye, see the...

- Bronze altar in the outer court and the bronze laver behind it
- Golden lampstand on the left in the inner court, the

table of showbread to the right, and the altar of incense straight ahead
• The Ark of the Covenant in the Holy of Holies

Do you see how these six pieces of furniture are in the shape of a *CROSS?* What is the picture God wants us to see in this? The entire Tabernacle is a representation of Jesus Christ! He is revealed in each piece of furniture, and when all of these separate pieces are seen in their totality, He is revealed as crucified on our behalf.

But notice that it requires *all* six pieces of furniture to form the Cross. From the bronze altar in the outer court to the Ark of the Covenant in the Holy of Holies, each one is necessary. If we stop at the bronze laver in the outer court, we don't have the full picture. If we stop at the golden altar of incense in the inner court, we may have a more accurate representation of Jesus, but the picture isn't complete.

What's the pattern?

In order to receive the fullness of Jesus' redeeming work on the Cross, we *must* enter into the Holy of Holies and experience the intimacy of God's presence. It's not enough to be saved. It's not enough to be baptized. It's not enough to be illumined by the Word on a daily basis, take communion, or even pray and worship. We *must* abandon ourselves fully to God and offer our lives as a living sacrifice to Him in the Holy of Holies. Anything less denies the fullness of what Jesus died to give us.

So how do we press into God's presence? How do we deepen the intimacy of our relationship with Him? How do we abide in the Holy of Holies?

The answer to these questions is simple, but it isn't necessarily easy, and it most certainly isn't popular. Like the rich young ruler who went away sad when Jesus told him what would be required of him in order for him to have eternal life (Matthew 19:15-26), many Believers shrink back when they learn what is required for us to have an intimate relationship with the Lord.

The tragic truth is that most of the world will *not* be saved, and most of us who *do* become Believers won't choose to press into an intimate relationship with the Lord. As Jesus said, *"For the gate is small and the way is narrow that leads to life, and there are few who find it"* (Matthew 7:14). But this doesn't have to be you!

SIX HABIT-FORMING PRINCIPLES

If you're one of the precious few who is choosing to press into God's presence, then I have **SIX PRINCIPLES** to share with you. These principles will help you develop Godly habits leading you to a more intimate relationship with Him.

Principle # 1: HAVE A DEDICATED TIME

Having a dedicated time each day to spend with the Lord is the first principle for forming the habit of being alone with Him. For me, the best time of day is in the morning. For you, it may be during your lunch break, or maybe it's the last hour of the day. The time of day doesn't really matter. What matters is consistency. Choose a time of day to be with God, and then stick to it. Make a daily appointment with Him, and then keep it. Of course schedules change, and there may be days when your regular quiet time simply isn't possible, but this should be the exception rather than the rule.

Principle # 2: HAVE A SPECIAL PLACE

The second principle for forming the Godly habit of being alone with Him is having a special place for your quiet time. Decide where your "Holy of Holies" will be, and then go there every day so that He can *"meet with you and speak with you"* there (Exodus 25:22). My special place to be alone with the Lord is in the study of our home. You may prefer a special chair in a corner somewhere, or maybe you have a sunny spot where you like to sit. It doesn't really matter, so long as it's a place that's quiet and peaceful for you.

Principle # 3: BE FREE FROM INTERRUPTIONS

A third principle for developing the habit of entering into God's presence on a daily basis is making sure that your time with Him is at a time and place that's free from interruptions. We all know what it's like to be in the middle of a conversation with someone whose cell phone rings, and they stop talking to us to answer the call. When this happens, we feel as though we really didn't have their attention, what we were saying was insignificant, or that we're not very important to them.

In the same way, when we're easily distracted by ringing phones, buzzing doorbells, or whining dogs, we're communicating to the Lord that we're not really paying attention to Him. Our time with Him needs to be focused, directed, and uninterrupted.

Principle # 4: LET THE HOLY SPIRIT DICTATE YOUR BODY AND SOUL

Habits are hard to form, but they're very easy to break. I heard someone say once that it takes three weeks to form a habit. While I don't know whether or not that's true, I do know from experience that it only takes a single day to break a good habit. My point is that while we can be devoted to developing the habit of seeking God's presence, we must be aware that this is one habit the enemy does *not* want us to form. He will try all sorts of tricks to make us a break the habit of spending meaningful time alone with God each day.

Which brings me to the fourth principle...

There will be days when we don't *feel* like entering into His presence to be alone with Him. Count on it. When we're stressed, overtired, too busy, really upset, or just plain out of sorts, spending time with the Lord and worshipping Him may be the very *last* thing we feel like doing. But this is actually when we need to be with Him the *most*.

On days like this, we can't base our decision of whether or not to spend an intimate quiet time with the Lord on soulish feelings. We must allow the Holy Spirit through our spirit dictate to our body and soul that we WILL spend time in His presence, regardless of whether we feel like it or not!

Principle # 5: SPEND MEANING-FULL TIME WITH THE LORD

If we desire intimacy with someone, we must be willing to invest **meaningful** time into the relationship. This is true if it's a relationship between a husband and a wife, a parent and a child, or two friends, and it's especially true if we want an intimate relationship with God.

For time spent with God to be meaningful, it must be "full of meaning" for both Him and me. It must be valuable. It must cost me something. Like King David, we shouldn't offer God what cost us nothing (1 Chronicles 21:24). If the time we spend with the Lord isn't meaningful to us, we can't expect it to be meaningful to Him.

Spending meaningful time in God's presence is a choice... it's a decision...it's a response to His invitation as He calls you to *"come away"* and be alone with Him (Song of Solomon 2:10). As you respond to the promptings of His Holy Spirit, your time alone with Him will be meaning-full.

Principle # 6: BEGIN AT THE BRONZE ALTAR BUT END UP IN THE HOLY OF HOLIES

Throughout this book, I've reminded you of the five words the Lord spoke to my spirit in that hotel coffee shop many years ago:

"REPENT. PRAISE. WORSHIP. OFFERING. SACRIFICE."

Although I was unaware that morning of the journey on which I was about to embark, God has faithfully led me on the pathway leading to His presence by revealing the pictures, patterns and mysteries of Moses' Tabernacle and Solomon's Temple. Through the years, He has deepened my knowledge and understanding of how these five words directly relate to what happens in the outer court, the inner court, and the Holy of Holies.

But He also has revealed something else to me....

Every day when I *"come away"* to spend some quiet time with Him, these five words are themselves the pathway leading me into His presence! Keep in mind that this isn't a formula for intimacy with God; it's simply the pattern He's given us to follow.

I begin with repenting for my daily sins...I gratefully praise Him for what He has done, is doing, and will do in my life and in the lives of my loved ones...in humility and awe, I worship Him for who He is...I offer myself to Him with abandon...and I trustingly give myself to Him as a living sacrifice.

We can't do this by ourselves. We need God's help to repent. Without His grace, our flesh doesn't *want* to praise and worship Him. Without His strength, we'll be too selfish to offer ourselves to Him with abandon and too afraid to die daily as a living sacrifice to Him.

However, with God's help, grace, and strength, we are able to gladly and willingly lay before Him all of our time, talent, and treasure...all of *ourselves*...for the sake of experiencing an intimate relationship with Him and for the joy of having His presence in our life.

IN HIS PRESENCE

Contrary to what we may have learned in Sunday school, we can't become intimate with the Lord simply by praying and reading His Word. All we end up with is head knowledge. You may win Bible Trivia contests with all you know "about" Him. But it's possible in all your "knowing" about Him to one day discover you don't really

Without His grace, our flesh

doesn't want to praise and

worship Him. Without His

strength, we'll be too selfish

to offer ourselves to Him with

abandon and too afraid to die

daily as a living sacrifice to Him.

"know" Him. We only truly get to know Him and experience genuine intimacy with Him when we're spending time in His presence.

And my friend, when we come before God cleansed from our sin... when we come before Him with our praises...when we come before Him in worship...when we come before Him as an offering...when we come before Him as living sacrifices...something wonderful happens...

God's presence comes! His love surrounds us! His glory covers us! His peace envelops us! And our spirit is one with His in intimacy.

The wonderful thing about God's presence is that anything... *anything*...can happen in our intimate times with Him. We can be...

- Forgiven!
- Reconciled!
- Healed!
- Freed!
- Restored!
- Transformed!

When we're with Him, there is nothing else we need. His love is sufficient, and it's His love that is calling us to press in to a deeper, more intimate relationship with Him.

There's a simple worship song I appreciate so much that describes His amazing love for us...a love that draws us to passionately pursue the pathway leading to His presence. It's called "Oh How He Loves You and Me."

Oh how He loves you and me,
Oh how He loves you and me;
He gave His life, what more could He give?
Oh how He loves you,
Oh how He loves me,
Oh how He loves you and me.
Jesus to Calvary did go,
His love for mankind to show;

What He did there brought hope from despair
Oh how He loves you,
Oh how He loves me,
Oh how He loves you and me.

–KURT KAISER, 1975

My friend, what Paul so clearly told the Christians living in Rome thousands of years ago is still true for us today:

"Who will separate us from the love of Christ? Will tribulation, or distress, or persecution, or famine, or nakedness, or peril, or sword?... But in all these things we overwhelmingly conquer through Him who loved us.

"For I am convinced that neither death, nor life, nor angels, nor principalities, nor things present, nor things to come, nor powers, nor height, nor depth, nor any other created thing, will be able to separate us from the love of God, which is in Christ Jesus our Lord" (Romans 8:35-39).

Oh how He loves you and me!

MY PRAYER FOR YOU

I'd like to encourage you today in your journey toward intimacy with the Lord. Let me pray for you...

Lord God, Thank You so much for the blood of your Son that covers us. Thank You that because of His death on the Cross, we can boldly approach Your throne of grace in time of need. In Jesus' Name, we **REPENT** *for those things we've done that have not glorified You, and we repent for the things we failed to do in obedience to You.*

God, we **PRAISE** *You for Who You are and what You are doing in our lives. Thank You that Your love will not let us go. Thank You that You have redeemed us and are leading us on the pathway to your presence.*

We **WORSHIP** *You because You are God and You are good. You* *are faithful and true. There is no other god beside You. You alone are worthy to receive all glory and honor and power and praise. Hallelujah!*

Lord God, we give ourselves to You as an **OFFERING.** *We lay before You our time, our talent, and our treasure. We hold nothing back. Like King David, we say that everything in the heavens and earth is Yours, O Lord, and this is Your kingdom. All that we have and all that we are, are Yours.*

We offer ourselves to You as a living **SACRIFICE,** *and we choose to die daily that You might live through us.*

God, let this be a day of new beginnings for my friend who is praying this prayer with me right now. May today be a turning point in their relationship with You. In the name of Jesus, release the blessing of a 100-fold relationship with You. Release a new hunger and a new passion for Your presence.

In Jesus' Name, make Your child forever discontent to remain in the outer court and even the inner court. By Your grace, help them to boldly come into the Holy of Holies. Lord, let your precious one dwell there...live there... camp there in Your presence before Your altar in worship of You. May Your child's life be a sweet-smelling fragrance before You.

Thank You God, that according to Your Word, You will meet with us and speak with them in this holy place. We bless You, God, in Jesus' name. Amen.

"Oh how He loves you and me,

Oh how He loves you and me;

He gave His life, what more could He give?

Oh how He loves you."

PRESS IN!

My friend, there's one last thought I want to share with you...

There is a process to developing intimacy with the Lord. It's one thing to know Him as Savior and to experience the joy of salvation in the 30-fold outer court. But it's a different thing altogether to press into a deeper, more intimate relationship with Him found in the 100-fold relationship of the Holy of Holies that He desires to have with us.

In any relationship, intimacy doesn't happen overnight. It takes time to create an intimate relationship with the Lord. Know that God's love is drawing you in, and He is cheering you on. Be patient with yourself in the process, knowing that He is patiently waiting for *you*.

The cry of Paul's heart was that he would *"know Him and the power of His resurrection"* (Philippians 3:10). Today, may this be the cry of your heart as well. May God give you the hunger, courage, and faith to respond to His love and press into the Holy of Holies. May you passionately pursue the pathway leading to His presence and abide there with Him forever.

Press in!

PART V

Ministry Resources

Inspiration
PROMISE BOOK

This beautiful, plush-covered, 242-page book is a

- Guide to help you pray for your loved ones
- Daily Devotional tool to bring you closer to the Lord
- Powerful manual for spiritual warfare

Do You Need a MIRACLE from God?

God is a God of MIRACLES!

Do you need God's supernatural intervention today in your...

- BODY, SOUL, OR SPIRIT?
- FINANCES, HOME, OR JOB?
- RELATIONSHIPS WITH LOVED ONES?

This life-changing ministry resource will help you experience the miracle you need from Him!

Get ready to receive YOUR miracle!

"How to Receive Your Miracle tells me how to look forward to God's promises for complete healing in my life. This book has been an eye opener for me to the keys of living!" — KAREN

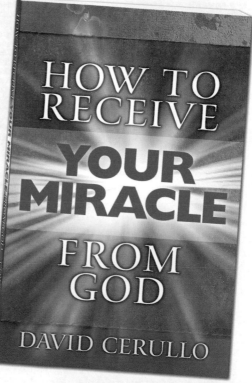

HOW TO RECEIVE YOUR MIRACLE FROM GOD

DAVID CERULLO

Sow a Seed for Souls and receive one or more of these with us to impact people for Christ worldwide!

HOPE FOR *Your* NEW BEGINNING

God wants to step into the circumstances of your life with His supernatural breakthroughs!
If you need a New Beginning in your...

Marriage • Job
Health • Finances
Children

...Hope For Your New Beginning book and audio CD will provide the tools you need to experience victory and abundance in Christ.

"I was blessed by your book New Beginnings. This is such a profound word from the heart of God, and I have asked the Lord to order my steps into His New Beginning. I want all the miracles and new beginnings He has ordained for my life and for my family's life this year and for years to come." — INGRID

Visit *Inspiration.org*, or call 866-324-5001 to ministry tools as a "Thank You" gift for partnering

CHOICES AND REWARDS

How to Live the Life God Loves to Bless

Do you ever wonder...

- Can God redeem your poor choices of the past?
- Do my daily choices matter to God?
- Am I doing enough for God's Kingdom?
- Are there Heavenly rewards based on my earthly choices?

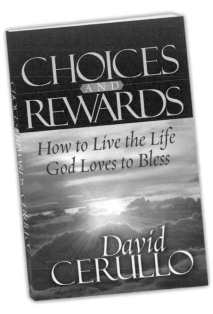

Choices and Rewards answers all of these questions and more. Receive teaching, encouragement, and inspiration to help you experience a new level of joy as you serve the Lord each day!

"Choices and Rewards was very inspiring and has made a great impact on me makig the right choices in my life! Thank you." — **SHIRLEY**

Sow a Seed for Souls and receive one or more of these with us to impact people for Christ worldwide!

"BATTLE FOR YOUR LIFE" VICTORY PACK
Will Give You the Tools You Need to Triumph Over the Enemy!

This powerful array of spiritual resources includes:

- *Battle for Your Life.* This timely manual will equip you to pull down enemy strongholds so you can discover God's destiny for your life!

- **Three video DVDs** of a teaching series on spiritual warfare. You'll want to watch the DVDs with your family, small group, or Sunday school class.

- **The audio CDs** of messages are a wonderful resource to listen to in your car, helping you put on the *"full armor of God"* each day!

- **A bookmark** to remind you of key Biblical principles for gaining victory over Satan. Keep it in your Bible or in your copy of the *Battle for Your Life* book!